FROMAJADAS
AND
INDIGO

Punta des Curbaio

C. don Nato

Cala Morel

Fontenellas

C. de Toro

C. de Somerider

Enfosias

Cala Colibre

Cala Laraho

Cap Bajoly

T. Bascos

Son Salamo

Cotolla

TERMINO

Villanor

Tour de Vante Ecuetia

Torre del Ram

Sonfé

Bou Atrama

Salecia

Sta. Agata

Ciudadela

Se Mulaina

T

Ance Dexal

Eliago

Ses Angoxas

Refel don Morra

DE

TERMINO DE

Ferena

St. Andria

Torre Trancade

Son Olivao

CIUDADELA

Son Olivart

TERURIA

Sona Parets

Son Jouit

Son Joan

Granada

C. der Touch

Son Marquet

Son Tora

Son More de Bax

Se Ma

Ance Marquet

Platges de Son Saura

T. B.

Ron

Cala Taquelouit

Cala Macarela

St. Caldona

Cala Tribaluc

C. del Ponente

R. de Son Bax

Cala

ISLE

MINORQUE

a Paris Chez Crepy.

1   2   3

FROMAJADAS

AND

INDIGO

The Minorcan Colony in Florida

KENNETH H. BEESON JR.

H
THE
History
PRESS

Published by The History Press
Charleston, SC 29403
www.historypress.net

Cover illustration and all internal line drawings are taken from *The Forgotten Isles: Impressions of Travel in the Balearic Isles, Corsica and Sardinia* by Gaston Vuillier. (English translation by Frederic Breton, 1896.)
Maps courtesy of the *St.* Augustine Historical Society.
Author photo courtesy of Alexis Beeson.

First published 2006
Second printing 2008

ISBN 978-1-5402-2463-7

Library of Congress Cataloging-in-Publication Data

Beeson, Kenneth H., d. 2003.
Fromajadas and indigo : the Minorcan colony in Florida / Kenneth H. Beeson.
p. cm.
Originally presented as author's thesis (Master's).
Includes bibliographical references.
ISBN 1-59629-113-3
1. Minorcans--Florida--Saint Augustine Region--History--18th century. 2. Minorcans--Florida--Saint Augustine Region--Economic conditions--18th century. 3. Plantations--Florida--Saint Augustine Region--History. 4. Indigo industry--Florida--Saint Augustine Region--History. 5. Saint Augustine Region (Fla.)--History. 6. Florida--History--English colony, 1763-1784. 7. Florida--History--Spanish colony, 1784-1821. I. Title.
F319.S2B44 2003
975.9'18--dc22
2005036375

Contents

Notes on Publication

The Menorcan Cultural Society is proud to support the publication of Kenneth H. Beeson's *Fromajadas and Indigo: The Minorcan Colony in Florida*. Originally a master's thesis, this manuscript has become a valued tool for scholars and researchers and is considered one of the best resources for study of the Minorcan culture. For that reason, and because Mr. Beeson passed away in 2003 and this publication is posthumous, the Board of Directors of the Menorcan Cultural Society has chosen to publish the manuscript in its original form, without additional changes or corrections.

The reader will notice a difference in spelling of Minorcan/Menorcan in this publication: Menorcan is the Spanish spelling and Minorcan is the English spelling. You will also note that there are references in the body of the work to several appendices. These included a typescript copy of a New Smyrna contract written in Spanish, and a partial listing of Father Camps's Register of Births, also referred to as the "Golden Book of the Minorcans." These two appendices have been left out of this publication due to space constraints. For scholars or genealogists interested in this information, an original copy of this manuscript with the appendices is available for viewing at the St. Augustine Historical Society Research Library in St. Augustine, Florida.

The Menorcan Society wishes to thank the Beeson family for allowing the original manuscript to be published. Thanks are also due to Carol Lopez-

Bradshaw, president of the Menorcan Society; Charles Tingley of the St. Augustine Historical Society Research Library; and Dr. Patricia Griffin and Dr. Dan Schafer for their advice. A special thank you to Merry Thomas, Danielle Bonfanti, Peggy and Robert Tibbs and Dr. Melanie Brown for their help in making this project a reality.

The Menorcan Cultural Society would also like to thank board member Sandie A. Stratton. Sandie, while completing a B.A. in history at the University of North Florida, spent hundreds of hours digitizing the original typewritten manuscript. She also helped conceive the cover and prepared all of the illustrations for the book. Sandie's dedication and passion for Mr. Beeson's work, from start to finish, helped make this project possible.

All of the text that follows is from the original manuscript completed by Kenneth Beeson in 1960.

Preface

To my mother and her Minorcan ancestors.

Fromajadas has many meanings to the numerous descendents of the Minorcan colony living in St. Augustine, Florida. The most common understanding is that it is a small pastry filled with cheese and customarily eaten during the Easter time. Almost every family of Minorcan descent knows the wonderful taste of the Fromajadas.

The Fromajadas is also a song, a Minorcan folk song. It was sung by bands of roaming singers in the streets. They would approach a house, sing a few verses, and expect to receive in return for their serenade a few Fromajadas. It was traditionally sung during the Easter time, especially on the eve of Easter Sunday. The first verse of the Fromajadas is as follows:

San Gabriel
Qui portaba la ambasciada,
Des nostro Rey del cel,
Estaran vos Prenada
Ya omilida
Tu ovavais aqui servanta
Fra del Deo Contenta
Para fa lo que el vol.

This tells of the announcement of the angel to Mary that she is to be the Mother of God. The remainder of the song narrates the grief of the Mother of Jesus during His passion and death. There is a transcription of the Fromajadas made by Howard Manucy and L. Hosmer. Had it not been for these two gentlemen the song might have been forgotten.

The Fromajadas, during the early days of the Minorcans' residence in St. Augustine, was also a form of trick or treat. During the feast days, roaming bands of Minorcan youths would approach a house, knock at the door, and if they were not offered anything to eat, they would perform a trick on the people of the residence.

Indigo was the crop that first offered a livelihood to the Minorcan settlers at New Smyrna. Without this merchantable crop the monetary returns from the colony's produce would not have been as large as they were. The colony itself was founded on the idea of producing large amounts of silk, though there is no record that any silk was ever produced at New Smyrna. The culture of the indigo plant and the manufacture of indigo, however, must have produced many skilled Minorcan workers.

The settlement of Dr. Turnbull at New Smyrna has left an indelible impression on the city of St. Augustine, for here remain many descendents of the Minorcan and Italian settlers. Many of the customs, food dishes, and a vocabulary, words of which may be spoken at any time during a normal conversation between people of Minorcan descent, remain very much alive today. The Fromajadas, the food dish called pilau (pronounced per-low), and the Minorcan word *troña* (meaning a pest or worrisome person) are commonplace, even in my own home. My children have adopted these Minorcan expressions, and they use them as part of their everyday speech.

I am most deeply indebted to the Saint Augustine Historical Society for giving me all possible assistance in making this study. The Society made all its facilities available to me at any time of the day or night. I especially want to thank Mrs. Doris C. Wiles, the librarian at the Historical Society Library for the help she gave me. Mr. J. Carver Harris, Mr. Albert Manucy, and Mr. X.L. Pellicer have been of more assistance than I am able to tell. These gentlemen even made a microfilm reader available for my use at home.

I am likewise indebted to Mr. Julian C. Younge and Miss Margaret Chapman of the Library of Florida History, for the kind assistance they have given me in preparing this thesis. They were more than helpful in assisting me to gather material and encouraging this study.

I am more than grateful to Dr. Donald E. Worcester, chairman of my supervisory committee. This gentleman was the person most responsible for the writing of this thesis. His encouragement began more than ten years ago.

Preface

Without his attention, assistance, and enthusiastic encouragement, this study would probably not have been made.

My gratitude is further extended to Mr. Harry Shaffer and Dr. Charles W. Arnade, who were kind enough to read some of the chapters of this thesis, and to give me constructive criticism.

I am sincerely grateful, and deeply indebted to my good friend, Mr. Luis R. Arana, for the help he offered in preparing this manuscript.

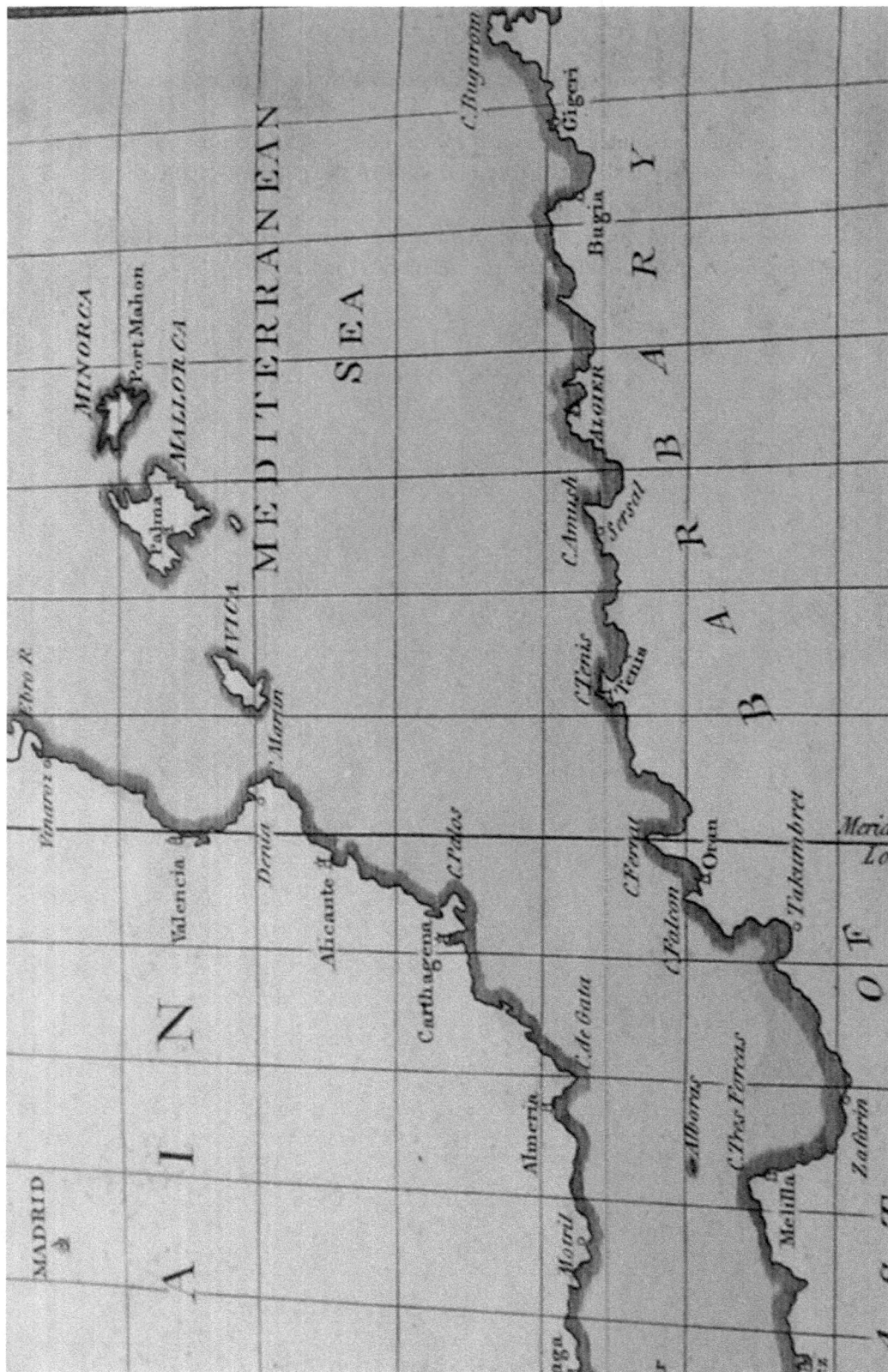

MADRID

S P A I N

Ebro R.

Vinarez

Valencia

Denia

Alicante

Carthagena

C. Palos

Almeria

C. de Gata

Motril

Alboras

Melilla

C. Tres Forcas

Zafarin

MINORCA
Port Mahon

MALLORCA

Palma

IVICA

MEDITERRANEAN

SEA

C. Bugarom

Gigeri

Bugia

ALGIER

B A R B A R Y

C. Amush

Sersal

C. Tenis

Tenis

C. Ferrat

C. Falcon

Oran

Takumbret

G U L F O F

Meridi
Lo

Introduction

The eighteenth century was the "Age of Enlightenment." It was a century of war, revolution, discontent, and empirical thought. The middle class was rising and the nobility was declining. In Europe, politically, the national state was clearly the most significant form of organization. The city-states were losing power. In the social class structure of Europe a new class was gaining importance, a middle class. It was composed of professional men like doctors and lawyers, merchants and bankers, who used their capital to make more money, industrialists who employed ten to hundreds of workers in shops and factories, or who sent out work to be done in the laborers' homes. The middle class was well-to-do and in general well educated. This class had economic power, but it enjoyed little political power or prestige Social status was still reserved for the upper classes that owned large estates.

Economically, Europe was exploiting, largely by means of commerce regulated by mercantilist principles, vast overseas areas in the Americas, in the Far East, and to a lesser degree in Africa. Money had now become important. From central Europe westward even serfs and peasants tended to pay dues in money rather than in labor and goods. Capitalism was well developed in commerce and finance. Industry was still mostly small-scale, though there were some large factories and mines. The guilds were disappearing, especially in

England. Machinery was being used more and the type of machinery used in manufacturing was becoming more complicated.

In agriculture, England made great strides. An "Agricultural Revolution" came into being. Root crops were introduced and made it possible to feed more cattle in the winter months, and to supply fresh meat throughout the year. There was an increase in the acreage of land under cultivation. Much attention was given to the draining of fens and marshes, to the breaking up and cultivating old, rough, common pastures, and to the hedging of land. The land was made more productive for both crops and livestock. To make the land more productive crop rotation was developed and farm machinery was being used.[1]

Science made great strides in the better understanding of nature. One of the greatest scientists of the century was Sir Isaac Newton (1642–1727). While Newton's work overshadows the other scientific developments of the time, these too were of tremendous scope and importance. Great strides were made in the invention and use of scientific instruments. The telescope and the microscope were perfected. The barometer, the air pump, the mercury thermometer, and the pendulum clock were developed. Experiments with static electricity led to the construction of the Leyden jar in which it can be stored.

The scientists, using the new devices, made many discoveries in many fields. Robert Boyle brought forth his law of the variation of the volume of gases under pressure, and aided in the separation of modern chemistry from alchemy. Malpighi confirmed Harvey's theory of the circulation of blood by observing capillary circulation with a microscope. Leewenhoek discovered protozoa and bacteria. Linnaeus set up a system of classification of plants, and Buffon, of animals. Halley calculated the orbit of the comet of 1682 and predicted correctly that it would return in 1759.

Science became fashionable and the talk of the day among the intellectuals of Europe and the colonies. Science even began to dominate the philosophical thought of the day and changed religious thought. The new philosophy was defined as "materialistic" and tried to explain everything in the universe in terms of matter and motion, and of forces that could be detected by the human senses. The English thinker, Thomas Hobbs, insisted that everything, including the human soul, must be understood in terms of matter and motion. Baruch Spinoza of Amsterdam set forth a philosophy called "pantheism." Gradually there developed a body of religious thought that is called "deism." Deists denied the divinity of Christ and all particularly Christian tenets of faith. Most of the advanced thinks of the century were deists, though some of the intellectuals remained devoutly Christian and fought the deists with the pen. The foremost of the enlightened thinkers in France was Francois Arouet (1694–1778), better known by his pen name Voltaire. His writings were witty and persuasive. He

Introduction

pleaded for rationalism, for the rule of nature. Soon rationalism gave way and a new philosophy of religious thought came into existence. By the end of the century there was a current of atheism as well as deism. The very existence of God was soon questioned. Secret societies, like the Freemasons, sprang up to further the cause of deism. Beginning in England, the Freemasons soon had lodges all over Europe.

On the other hand, new branches of the Christian faith came forth. An Englishman, George Fox, founded a sect that became popularly known as the "Friends," or "Quakers." Most were humble folk, though some were aristocratic, such as William Penn, the founder of Pennsylvania. John Wesley led a group of students that came to be nicknamed the "Methodists."

To combat the movements of the enlightened thinkers of the century, the Roman Catholic Church worked night and day through the members of the Society of Jesus. So vigorous and successful were the Jesuits in replying to the "philosophes" that they were singled out for the most virulent attacks by the rationalists. The latter found allies among the absolute sovereigns of the age, who felt themselves more enlightened than the Jesuits. It was this century that saw the Jesuits driven out of Portugal, France, Spain, and all other Spanish possessions. The absolute sovereigns went so far in their drive that Pope Clement XIV was prevailed upon to decree the formal suppression of the Society of Jesus.

The eighteenth century began with the War of the Spanish Succession and ended with the rise of an ambitious little Corsican named Napoleon Bonaparte. England and Spain, our principals in this study, were embroiled in war throughout the entire period. These wars began on the continent of Europe and gradually moved across the vast expanses of the Atlantic Ocean onto the continent of North America. Trade, commerce, and territorial expansion on the part of the mother countries seemed to be the primary causes of conflict in the colonies.

Meanwhile, the continent of Europe was making manufactured goods. In the colonies the peoples were still trading with the Indians and living a somewhat remote life. An urban culture was beginning to take shape on the two continents of the Americas, and in the English colonies an American culture was appearing. The first newspaper, the *Boston News-Letter*, appeared in 1704. The demand for books grew also and employed an increasing number of printers in turning out American editions of English works. Libraries sprang up; the Library Association of Philadelphia was founded in 1731, chiefly through the efforts of Benjamin Franklin. Yale University came into existence in 1701. Princeton University dates from 1746, and the University of Pennsylvania was founded in 1755. In the field of science Benjamin Franklin won international fame.

Theatrics cannot be overlooked. The first theatre was built at Williamsburg in 1716, and New York also had a playhouse. In addition, Americans bought books, and read and wrote books.

On the continent of South America, Spain's colonies had been in existence much longer than those of England in North America. Here too existed a culture typically colonial. A university was founded in Santo Domingo as early as 1538. The University of Santiago de la Paz or Gorjón opened in 1558. The University of San Marcos in Lima opened in 1571, and the University of Mexico in 1553. Many books were written in America during the sixteenth century alone, on many subjects. Columbus himself may have begun the literature of America with his *Journals*. Drama, art, architecture and poetry were also produced. They were far older than those originating in the English colonies to the north.

The eighteenth century was by no means lacking in power politics. War is a phenomenon of politics, to be understood as regards its cause and course and cure within the context of specifically political motives and practices. In 1756, the Seven Years' War began, involving England, Spain, and France as the principals. A number of problems existed on the international scene, and to settle them the war ensued. Some of the problems were: whether France or England was to rule India; whether French or English manners, language, and institutions were to prevail over the immense continent of North America; whether Germany was to a have a national existence; whether Spain was to monopolize the tropics; who was to command the ocean; who was to be dominant in the islands of the Spanish American waters; what power was to possess the resources and markets of the globe.

The struggle came to the North American continent and is known as the French and Indian War, a most misleading title to say the least. It was the latter phase of this war that cost Spain her last foothold on the North American continent, Florida. In the struggle that followed the strategic port of Havana, Cuba was captured by the English. The English also captured Manila as an added prize. With these events Spain was placed in a most awkward position. She could not afford to lose Havana, and Manila had cost her a considerable amount of money and blood to build. The Treaty of Paris 1763 called for negotiations to settle Spain's problem and position.

At this point Spain was ready to negotiate to the utmost. To the victor belongs the spoils, but it was not too late to spoil the victor. The result of the treaty was that Spain was given back Havana and Manila, and England took Florida in exchange. England also received all Spanish and French possessions east of the Mississippi River. England also received a monopoly of lumber rights in Honduras.

Introduction

Spanish rule in Florida was now ended. Florida had been Spanish since 1565, and now the Spanish language was to live only among the remaining Indios Christianos. For the first time the English flag flew from Canada to the Everglades, and all along the eastern side of the Mississippi River. In order to compensate Spain for her losses, France gave her all French possessions west of the Mississippi as well as New Orleans. In addition to removing Spain from the southern extremities of the English colonies of North America, England also solved the Anglo-French contest for supremacy in North America and placed France in a state of bankruptcy. England was now undisputed mistress of the seas and George III was the leading monarch of the day.

Power politics at the very beginning of the century had cost Spain some territory. The War of the Spanish Succession (1701–1714)(Queen Anne's War on the North American Continent), enflamed the entire continent of Europe, though Spain herself was the principal battleground. In 1704, England seized Gibraltar from Spain. On September 30, 1708, the island of Minorca fell into English hands, to remain an English possession for nearly a century. At the treaty of Utrecht, 1713: Gibraltar and Minorca were ceded to England; by the asiento or compact, England was granted the monopoly of importing Negro slaves into Spanish America for thirty years; English merchants were accorded the right of sending one ship a year to Spanish American ports. Spain also surrendered the Catholic Netherlands, Milan, Naples and Sardinia to Austria, and the island of Sicily to Savoy. The asiento and the right of English merchant vessels to enter Spanish American ports made this phase of the treaty a veritable entering wedge for English commerce in the Spanish colonies.

Minorca, though a possession of England, had been culturally related to the Spanish province of Catalonia for centuries. Catalonia had long been a nation so far as language and institutions are concerned. This province had always been a thorn in Spain's side for the Catalan were different. In 1468 and 1629 Catalonia revolted, and in 1640 formed a republic and made an alliance with France. In the War of the Spanish Succession (1705), Catalonia had favored the opposite side, the allies. In 1736, a body of Catalan patriots visited England to ask for fulfillment of the earlier English promise to maintain the fueros, but the English government ignored their petition.

Classifying a nation is not easy. We shall leave aside the original population and the inevitable visit of the Roman legions, and come to the Visigoths who, as we know, occupied what is now Catalonia in the fifth century and gave their name to the country. Catalonia is a corruption of Gothalania. Catalan, however, is distinctly a romance language, more so than Spanish, which still retains many words of Germanic etymology. It is a derivative of the Provençal, a language that is now a mere philological curiosity recently resurrected by the poet Mistral (1830–1914). Catalan, on the other hand, is a living tongue spoken by over four million people in Spain and the Balearic Isles, a situation that can be explained only by the fact that Catalonia was a fief of the Counts of Provence, the Berenguers. The association of the two provinces was therefore a close one until Raymond de Berenguer married the heiress to the crown of Aragon in 1137, after which Catalonia was absorbed by Spain while Provence drifted into the French camp after the marriage of Charles of Anjou with Beatrice de Berenguer. Provençal survived in a modified form in Catalonia but ultimately died out in France.[2]

When England took possession of Florida in 1763, the Spaniards of Florida retired to Cuba and Louisiana. In East Florida only eight Spaniards remained behind, and by 1764, even they left. All that remained were the buildings and the old Castillo de San Marcos to remind the English that Spain had been there. The Spanish continued to cause the English problems by fishing in Florida waters and occasionally landing in sheltered coves. These actions caused much unrest in the minds of the English officials and settlers. The Indians, too, were uneasy with the Spanish still in the area. The action on the part of Spain never amounted to more than fishing expeditions from Cuba and proved not to be a Spanish design on Florida.

With the depopulation of East Florida, the problem of colonizing and settling the territory became a prime necessity. During the administration of Governor Grant, the first English governor, an experiment in colonization was made. A land grant was given to Dr. Andrew Turnbull and his English associates. The Scottish Dr. Turnbull had lived some years in the Mediterranean countries. He became convinced that a colony consisting of people who were accustomed to a warm climate could raise crops as they had in their native lands. He was convinced that it would be a good business investment. In 1768, three equal grants of land consisting of twenty thousand acres each were awarded to Dr. Turnbull and his other two associates. These equal grants were to be operated jointly for seven years. The operating expense was not to exceed £9000. After receiving the grant, Turnbull went to East Florida to make a reconnaissance of his newly acquired land. He returned the same year and began to collect settlers for his enterprise. He went to Leghorn, Italy first and procured about one hundred and twelve Italians. He took the Italians to the island of Minorca and then went to Greece in search of more colonists. He brought the Greek settlers he was able to procure to the island of Minorca also. While in Minorca he procured settlers from the island itself.

This heterogeneous group was considerably larger than Turnbull had anticipated enlisting. Its size placed quite a burden upon the meager sustenance

18

found in East Florida initially. Nevertheless, the colony at New Smyrna was successful for a few years before trouble began. Turnbull broke openly with the governor of East Florida, Patrick Tonyn, and returned to England to plead his case with the Colonial Governor of the Province of East Florida. The colony at New Smyrna moved to St. Augustine during Turnbull's absence. This action was prompted by harsh and cruel treatment of the overseers of the colony. The settlers repudiated their contracts with Turnbull. Their movement from New Smyrna was encouraged and upheld by Governor Tonyn.

The colony began to move from New Smyrna to St. Augustine in 1776, the very year of the signing of the Declaration of Independence by the colonies to the north. The spirit of the times had finally moved into East Florida. The international movements were still at work, for prior to 1775, the Minorcans were discovered to be in communication with the Spanish at Havana. Revolt was rife in the colonies and the seeds of sedition had already been sown. Suspicion and fear dominated the period, and Spain was known to desire the recovery of the Floridas, for Florida was still the key to defense and control of the Bahama Channel.

This present study is of the colony itself. It is the story of my mother's maternal and paternal ancestors from the island of Minorca. Parts of the story were often told to me by my maternal grandmother. Her life began nearly one hundred years after the Minorcan envoys swam the Matanzas Inlet in search of relief from New Smyrna, and came to St. Augustine, Florida.

I.

Land Grant Policy
in English East Florida

The Seven Years' War officially came to an end on February 10, 1763, when the Treaty of Paris was signed. Spain ceded all her other possessions east of the Mississippi, as well as her claims to the New England fisheries, to England. There was much opposition to the peace, which roused a storm of protest throughout England. Bute, the English Prime Minister, was hissed and stoned as he went to and from Parliament, and was forced to hire a bodyguard of "bruisers and butchers" to protect him from the mobs. The English middle class was dissatisfied, for they felt that the military victories of England in the recent war warranted more favorable advantages than were given at the peace table. Spain had been defeated and Havana was rich, more so than Florida. The English middle class thought that corruption and intimidation were rife in Parliament. Dissatisfaction was so prevalent that on April 7, 1763, Prime Minister Bute resigned.[3] Such was the reception that the addition of Florida to the remaining colonies of England in North America received. Regardless of its reception, Florida was now English. A transition was about to take place and the English lost no time in occupying Florida. The Spanish occupation of Florida was now ended, for the time being. The date for the English to take formal possession of Florida was set for three months, or sooner, after ratification of the treaty.

Florida was soon divided into two separate provinces, East and West Florida.[4] The former, the principal concern of the present study, included the peninsula and the mainland west from the Atlantic coast to the Apalachicola River. Pensacola, Mobile, and the land between the Apalachicola and the Mississippi delta comprised West Florida, a combination of the territory ceded by both France and Spain.[5]

The first notification of the actual occupation by the English was made to the Spanish in St. Augustine, March 16, 1763, by Captain John Carey commanding H.M.S. *Bonetta*. He conveyed dispatches from the Governor of South Carolina concerning the articles of peace. Lieutenant Sandys was placed ashore and courteously received by the Spanish in the presidio.[6] Lieutenant Sandys then returned to the *Bonetta* and sailed away. On July 20, 1763, Captain Hodges,[7] commanding a Battalion of the First Regiment, English Expeditionary Force in Havana, arrived in St. Augustine aboard H.M.S. *Renoun*, and took possession.[8] The English occupation of East Florida then began with Captain Hodges the temporary military governor. Ten days after his arrival, Captain Hodges was replaced and his command was integrated into a newly arrived unit from Havana, the Ninth Regiment, commanded by Major Francis Ogilvie. Major Ogilvie arrived on July 30, 1763, and took formal command of East Florida with the full power of the English crown.[9]

The population of St. Augustine numbered 3,046 Spaniards and a regiment of English soldiers and officers.[10] England now introduced a policy quite different concerning the occupation of Florida. Spain had held Florida merely as an overseas military garrison complete with dependents. The presidio itself was dependent upon the viceroy of New Spain for subsistence and logistical support. England intended to transform the province into a colony, populated with agriculturists, not soldiers. The military garrison was to be stationed there to support the colony only in military matters. The colonists themselves were not in the pay of the king, unless they were there as a royal official. The colony had to learn to support itself, for it was now actually a business investment. An important function of the colony was to supply the mother country with raw materials for the factories that were beginning to come into existence.

The garrison in St. Augustine was soon to be left entirely to the English Ninth Regiment, which was billeted wherever room could be found for them. The officers were billeted in private homes, and the troops were quartered in the Castillo. All Spanish property in the town was put up for quick sale, for all but a few Spaniards, including Governor Feliu, had decided to leave Florida to the Protestant English, even though religious freedom had been granted them. Their idea was to sell their property immediately and leave for Cuba. The old presidio was then occupied by the Ninth Regiment and the eight Spaniards who remained in their midst. These eight Spaniards awaited the arrival of prospective English purchasers of the unsold Spanish property, which was considerable.

It is obvious the English were happy, in most respects, to see the Spanish population leave. Food was scarce, luxuries were few, and the major differences in religion, customs, and government would have caused many difficulties. The government was now simple. There was only Major Ogilvie, his command, eight Spaniards, and perhaps a few English civilians,[11] and it was not difficult to keep law and order within a military command. The eighteenth-century English army was capable of keeping order among its personnel. In addition, the Regimental Supply officer had an easy task, as it was a simple matter to requisition supplies for the command. Civilians, however, and particularly foreigners, involved serious logistical problems. The presence of foreign civilians in an occupied area would also require an additional staff officer, or additional duties for one already assigned, duty that would require the major portion of his time and effort in the conduct of military government. Thus the responsibilities of Major Ogilvie in regards to civilian government were relatively simple.

In the latter part of 1763, the Board of Trade transmitted the Proclamation of October to Major Ogilvie.[12] With the announcement of the Proclamation of October came also the forewarning that the military government was about to end. East and West Florida had been declared two separate provinces with two distinct governmental heads, completely independent of one another. The Proclamation clearly stated that emphasis would be placed upon settling Florida, Quebec, and Nova Scotia, and that civil governments, patterned after the usual colonial type, were to be instituted immediately to encourage settlers. The Proclamation also promised the settlers full benefit of English laws, and authorized the new governments to call assemblies, set up courts, and award land grants to settlers, with special benefits to ex-service men. The government established a policy of easy purchase terms for prospective settlers.[13]

Land grants could be obtained from either the Board of Trade in London or the governor of East Florida and his council in concert. The larger grants, of 20,000 acres in township tracts, were awarded by the Board of Trade. The smaller grants were awarded by the governor and his council.[14]

The Board of Trade stated publicly in 1763 that any who would undertake the settlement of land in East Florida at his own expense with the proper number of Protestant families from the colonies or other foreign ports, could obtain grants up to 20,000 acres provided the land was settled within ten years with one person for every 100 acres. The whole grant was subject to forfeiture if one-third of it was not settled within three years. Any part not settled at the end of ten years was also subject to forfeiture. There were restrictions regarding natural resources found within the grant. All mines of gold, silver, lead, and coal were the property of the king.[15]

The administrative procedure for obtaining a township grant from the Board of Trade was relatively simple. Persons desiring to make a settlement in East Florida were required to present a petition to the Privy Council in London. The petition was reviewed and, if approved, was forwarded to the Board of Trade for recommendations. The Board would then return the petition to the Privy Council and an order in Council was presented to the petitioner. The Order in Council was required to be presented by the petitioner, or a representative, to the governor of East Florida and his council. The governor and his council then issued a warrant of survey and subsequently made the grant on the terms stated in the Order in Council.[16]

It was relatively simple to obtain a land grant from the governor of East Florida and his council. A person who desired a grant was required merely to present a written petition directly to the governor. The governor and his council awarded two types of grants, a "family right" and the "king's bounty." These were the smaller types of grants. A petitioner qualified for a "family right" grant as the head of a family. He could obtain 100 acres of land, and an additional fifty acres for each man, woman, and child, black or white, in his family. He could also purchase up to 1,000 acres at five shillings for 50 acres, if he could prove satisfactorily that he could provide for its cultivation. A petitioner qualified for a "king's bounty" grant if he was a reduced pay Army or Naval Officer, or an honorably discharged ex-service person.[17] The land was subject to forfeiture, under both types of grants, unless three acres in fifty were cleared or otherwise developed within three years; however, legal proof of settlement of three acres in fifty gave permanent title to each fifty acres.[18]

A rent called the "quit rent" was imposed by the English government on all land grants. On land awarded by the Board of Trade the rent was a halfpenny per acre on half the land at the end of a five-year period, and a halfpenny per acre on the entire grant at the end of a ten-year period.[19] In the case of the "family right" grant, or "king's bounty" grant, the rent was a halfpenny per acre on the total grant of acreage at the end of a two-year period.[20]

On August 29, 1764, the military government of East Florida ended and the first governor of the new province, James Grant, arrived in St. Augustine aboard the sloop *Ferrat*.[21] Hereafter life in the colony would assume the complexion of business and experimentation designed for business. The government was prepared to function in East Florida, and all that was needed was someone to govern. The major problem was to populate the province of East Florida, and this was not easy.

Land Grant Policy in English East Florida

The English knew little about Florida or its climate, terrain, soil, and Indians. What was known had to be disseminated. A large-scale program of advertisement was needed, and the naturalists of the day, such as Bernard Romans and William Bartram, were happy to be of assistance. Settlers were slow in coming, though there were many speculators with visions of large land grants. Much information about Florida was given by the Indians, and a certain amount of information most certainly had to be given by the Spanish before their departure. To add to this information quite a few books and pamphlets were published to add fuel to the fire. Some of the works promoting interest in Florida were *The American Gazetteer* (London, 1762); Robert Rogers, *Concise Account of North America* (London, 1765); and William Roberts, *Account of the First Discovery, and Natural History of Florida* (London, 1763). Governor Grant himself did a considerable amount of advertising. He placed notices in all the English colonies and provinces.[22] He painted a beautiful picture of East Florida, describing the many advantages of settling in this tropical paradise. He even stated his liberal land grant policies.[23]

Whether or not the publicity campaign influenced settlers to come into East Florida is not certain. Today, in the twentieth century, we have no yardstick to measure the benefits of advertisement, so it is virtually impossible to suggest the amount of importance of this eighteenth-century publicity campaign. It is certain, however, that the land surveys aided in inducing settlers to come to East Florida. In the early period of Governor Grant's administration, many huge tracts were surveyed under the watchful eye of the controversial surveyor general of East Florida, a Dutch emigrant form Georgia, William Gerrard de Brahm. This gentleman, with several assistants including Bernard Romans, completed a survey of the coast of East Florida prior to publishing his now famous "Report."[24] The land was divided into tracts to be granted by the English government to prospective settlers, and to avoid future litigation. The government could then grant clear titles to the land.

The English government was pushing the sale of Florida real estate and a land "boom" was on. The land "boom" was not of the magnitude of the real estate boom in Florida in the 1920's, but it was important at any rate. Land speculation was popular among gentlemen of importance, rank, and wealth. In the year 1767 this group acquired 122 grants in East Florida alone.[25] A hasty glance at the total number of applicants for land grants in any of the newly acquired colonies clearly shows that East Florida was the major attraction. This was a period of intense speculation, particularly in the American colonies, and East Florida received a lion's share of interest.

Little or no interest was shown in actually settling the newly acquired province of East Florida, however, with the exception of the project under study and another by Denys Rolle at Rollestown, near the present site of Palatka, Florida. The number of land grants shows that the publicity campaign was successful, even though the actual colonization was slight.

There were, however, many English subjects who entertained the speculative idea of colonizing a township grant. In 1763 the Board of Trade received many petitions, but no colonies resulted. A.M. Vivegnis desired to establish a small arms munitions factory to supply the English army in America. His plan was to transport over 1,000 munitions workers from Liege. Dr. William Stork desired to settle a group of Germans. A Mr. McMutt petitioned the Board of Trade for permission to settle a colony of French Protestants.[26]

A most encouraging proposal was made in 1764 by a gentleman named John Savage who desired a harbor site for a settlement. He proposed to settle as many as 200 persons from Bermuda. He stated that his colony would most probably consist of more than 400, but he guaranteed at least 200. The purpose of the settlement was to establish a shipbuilding industry in East Florida. He even offered to pay five pounds per person. Governor Grant received this news enthusiastically. He offered a grant south of the Mosquetto Inlet.[27]

Lands on the banks of the St. Mary's and Nassau rivers were also desired by prospective settlers. In 1765 Ephrain and John Gilbert, also of Bermuda, petitioned Governor Grant for 20,000 acres each. The town of New Bermuda was planned after a survey by De Brahm, but was never settled. Plans called for 500 families. About 80 families from Bermuda arrived in Savannah in 1766, bound for New Bermuda, but they did not continue to the colony. Sickness and death discouraged this group. One of the Gilberts died, and the whole plan was abandoned.[28]

In 1767, a petition was presented to the Board of Trade on behalf of Antoine Louis de Norac, Chevalier Seigneur de la Tour Duprés de Wailly, for a township grant. His plan called for a colony of Swiss. In 1773 the Cape Florida Society requested 6,000 acres of Lord Dartmouth's grant to be settled by foreign families. This petition was made by four Swiss gentlemen, James Samuel Loup, J. James Benhole, Daniel Bercher, and Henry Dessoulavy. John Augustus Ernst, a German resident of England, desired a land grant to settle Protestants from Switzerland and Germany.[29]

By 1776, 16 grants were settled totaling 222,000 acres. This would indicate that progress was being made with regard to the colonization of East Florida. The 16 grantees were: Richard Gewald 20,000 acres; John Tucker 20,000 acres; Witter Cuming 5,000 acres; Peter Taylor 10,000 acres; Patrick Tonyn 20,000 acres; Francis Levett 10,000 acres; Andrew Turnbull 20,000 acres; Sir William Duncan 20,000 acres; William Knox 2,000 acres; Sir Edward Hawke 20,000 acres; Christopher Thornton 10,000 acres; Richard Russell 10,000 acres and Robert Bissett 5,000 acres.[30] Of the 16 grants that were settled, only two were of major importance—the settlement at Rollestown and the colony of Dr. Andrew Turnbull at Mosquetto Inlet.

Doctor Turnbull
and His Land Grant

A ndrew Turnbull was a Scottish physician practicing in London. In 1766 Dr. Turnbull was forty-eight years old and prosperous.[31] Prior to his resident practice in London, Dr. Turnbull served as a Consul for the English government in Smyrna, Greece. He had been in many places in the Levant and knew the Aegean and its islands well.[32] About 1751, Dr. Turnbull married Maria Gracia Dura Bin, the daughter of a wealthy Greek merchant of Smyrna.[33] A son, Nicholas, was born while the Turnbulls were stationed in Smyrna.[34]

Dr. Turnbull, in 1766, caught the fever of speculation. After much conversation on the subject with his wife and friends, Dr. Turnbull decided to abandon his medical practice in London and establish a Greek colony in East Florida. His colony would be established to raise silk worms, indigo, and cotton, just as the Greeks were doing in their native land. He knew the Greeks well, and considered them desirable colonists. He had traveled extensively in the Aegean and was well acquainted with the Greeks' food crops and agricultural produce.[35]

The doctor was a man of influence in London.[36] He was a personal friend of many men of wealth and influence, including the Earl of Shelburne, President of the Board of Trade.[37] From his group of friends and associates, Dr. Turnbull found a partner for his venture in East Florida, Sir William Duncan, a Baronet[38] and a Knight of the Garter.[39] Turnbull and Duncan filed a request for a township grant with the Board of Trade and approval of their request came through the

King in Council, June 17, 1776.[40] Two separate township grants of 20,000 acres each were given to Turnbull and Duncan. According to the Proclamation of October 1763, Turnbull or Duncan was required to present his orders from His Majesty in Council to the governor of East Florida. He would next select and survey the grant, and then make formal application for it through the Board of Trade in London. The surveyed land was then recorded and the deed was granted to the applicant by the king. After this the land could be physically occupied and the quit rent would commence.

In November 1766, Dr. Turnbull and family arrived in St. Augustine.[41] Turnbull presented to Governor Grant his orders from His Majesty in Council for two tracts of land of 20,000 acres each, one for Sir William Duncan and one for himself. The Governor issued warrants of survey to him, and aided him personally in his selection of land. Dr. Turnbull selected land on the Hillsborough River south of Mosquettos, a choice site.[42] It is not known when Dr. Turnbull actually named his grant, but it was undoubtedly soon after having the land surveyed. It is known, however, that he named it New Smyrna out of respect for the birthplace of his wife.[43] The name New Smyrna appears in every manuscript after his return from the reconnaissance and selection of his land site. This was to be the southernmost settlement in British East Florida.

Dr. Turnbull must have observed scenery that is typically tropical Florida, for from the Mosquettos south can be seen such tropical flora as carica, barassus, capsious, mangles and blackwood.[44] Human activity was already there in the form of a plantation owned by Mr. Fennan.[45] A Captain Bisset and a Mr. Oswald also had plantations there.[46]

Mosquetto Inlet and its environs were surveyed in 1765 by William Gerard De Brahm. He placed the Mosquetto inlet at latitude 25° 54' 00" east of St. Augustine, and 00° 38' 14 ½" east of the St. Mary's River. The bar's channel was then about 300 feet wide with over 10 ½ feet of water covering it at flood tide. The soundings increased gradually from 10 ½ feet in the bar's channel to 36 feet within the harbor. This would afford ample water for a sloop to sail over the bar with ease. The north stream, which is the Halifax River, offered at least 10 feet of water at all times. The south stream of Mukoso harbor, which is the Hillsborough River, offered at least the same amount of water. At the southern point of the inlet stood a high bluff overlooking the harbor. There were high sand hills on both the north and south sides measuring 2,900 links from north to south.[47]

Mr. De Brahm surveyed this area again in 1767. William Bartram was present at this survey, which was undoubtedly made for Dr. Turnbull.[48] There were neither habitations nor cleared fields in the future New Smyrna site, though there was a large orange grove on the south promontory of a ridge. The ridge was nearly a half a mile wide and stretched north for about 40 miles up to the head of the North Moscuetto, which united with the Tomoko River. This whole ridge was entirely covered with orange trees. Mingled with the orange trees were live oak, magnolias, palms, red bays, and many other varieties. It was a veritable jungle covered with vines and moss. Where the colony was to be located stood a spacious Indian mound and an avenue near the banks of the river. The avenue ran on a straight line back through the orange groves and across the ridge. It ended at the verge of natural savanna and ponds.[49]

In addition to selecting and having the two tracts of land surveyed, Dr. Turnbull also began preliminary preparations for the arrival of his colony. He purchased some Negro slaves, hired a skilled planter and an overseer, and began to clear his land to plant cotton. He purchased a large number of cattle from Georgia and Carolina and had them delivered to the Mosquettos. He hired artificers and began the construction of houses.[50]

Dr. Turnbull became a prominent figure while in East Florida, and was acquainted with some of the more important personalities in the Council. He seems to have been well liked, and his ideas were thought of as sound. His connections in London might have influenced his reception. At any rate, he most certainly had aroused the Governor with his plans and actions, for Governor Grant was most interested in anything that would help populate his province. The Governor's communications to his superior highly praised and admired the doctor's undertakings. Turnbull's conduct was called encouraging to every inhabitant in the province. His actions and plans induced the governor to remark, "if all gentleman who have obtained orders from His Majesty for land in this province act with the same spirit, East Florida will soon become a useful plantation to Great Britain." Requests were even made for a government subsidy to every settler brought to East Florida by the Governor.[51] The population of St. Augustine was about 3,000 at this time.[52] Governor Grant needed some assistance from London to prevent emigrants from leaving South Carolina, where a subsidy of four pounds sterling was given to every white emigrant. The governor also requested that a bounty be given to Dr. Turnbull for his settlers.[53]

The impression that Turnbull made on Governor Grant and the prominent planters of East Florida acquired for him an appointment on the East Florida Council. In January 1767 Dr. Turnbull was appointed Secretary of the Council, Clerk of the Crown, and Clerk of Common Pleas of the East Florida Council.[54]

By January 20, Dr. Turnbull was prepared to return to England.[55] He had accomplished much in the two months he was in East Florida. With his family well cared for in St. Augustine, his land being cleared at the Mosquettos, and cattle on the way from Georgia and South Carolina, Dr. Turnbull could relax on his voyage to England. In the latter part of January 1767, he left the province of East Florida and sailed for England.[56] Meanwhile, his formal request for his grant was approved in England. Grant number 40 was awarded to Andrew Turnbull Esq., consisting of 20,000 acres. The King's order was signed on January 17, 1767. Turnbull's quit rent was fixed at one half due on the Feast of St. Michael, 1772, and the other half due on the same date in 1777. Grant number 41 was awarded to Sir William Duncan, consisting of 20,000 acres. The King's order was signed on the same date as Turnbull's. Duncan's quit rent was fixed at one half due on the Feast of St. Michael, 1772, and the other half in 1777.[57]

Dr. Turnbull arrived in England before March, 1767.[58] Lord George Grenville, a third partner was added to his colonial enterprise shortly after his arrival in London.[59] To administer his investment in the enterprise Lord Grenville named a naval officer, Commander Richard Temple, to take full charge. Shortly after that, Commander Temple was granted 20,000 acres on behalf of Lord Grenville.[60]

Now that he had land in East Florida, Dr. Turnbull began in earnest to make preparations for the formation of his colony. For capital he had 24,000 pounds at his disposal, half of the amount from Sir William Duncan, and the other half from Lord Grenville.[61] All the preliminary preparations were being made for the arrival of 500 Greek colonists at the Mosquettos [62] Turnbull was assured of a position of prominence in East Florida by acquiring a seat on the East Florida Council, the governing body of the Province. Government assistance was also assured both from England and the Province of East Florida. Turnbull had all he needed with the exception of colonists. His next problem was to procure settlers and transport them to the Mosquettos. In order to advance his scheme, the Doctor had to arrange transportation to and from the Levant, and transportation costs were high.

Sometime in March, 1767, Turnbull addressed a petition to King George through the Board of Trade. He informed the king officially that he had recently returned from the Province of East Florida. He then notified the king that he found the soil and climate in East Florida suitable for raising cotton and silk production. He stated that he proposed to establish a colony of Greeks there to produce these articles, which he believed would induce many others to immigrate to the colonies. He asked for a decommissioned sloop-of-war to be converted into a transport and appointed for his use to transport the Greek colonists. Turnbull would be responsible for the expense of manning the vessel, provisioning it, and all other expenses that might be incurred. He needed this vessel badly.[63]

Doctor Turnbull and His Land Grant

Turnbull's petition was referred to the Board of Trade, the next higher authority in the chain of administration of the English Colonial Government. On April 7 the Lords of Trade, Clare, George Rice, Soame Jenyns, and Thomas Robinson gave their opinion to the President of the Board of Trade, the Earl of Shelburne. They stated that in their opinion a colony of Greeks engaged in the culture of silk and cotton would be of public utility. They saw no reason why Dr. Turnbull should not be given use of the vessel he petitioned for, provided that it be approved by the Minister of His Majesty's Navy. It was their further opinion that the issuance of the vessel would work no particular hardship on the Navy.[64] It does indicate, however, that the English government was prepared to be of assistance in this enterprise.

Turnbull then petitioned the crown for money. His petition in the form of a memorial was presented to the Board of Trade some time in April 1767. The Doctor reminded King George of the annual subsidy of 500 pounds granted by Parliament in 1764. This bounty was for encouraging the culture of cotton, vines, silk and other articles of commerce in East Florida. The subsidy had not yet been awarded to anyone in East Florida. Turnbull asked for it not only for the year 1767, but for 1766 and 1765 as well, a total of 1500 pounds. He said that the initial 1500 pounds would be a premium for bringing Greeks skilled in the culture of cotton, vines and silk into the Province. The 1500 pounds would be merely 3 pounds per person. If he were granted the annual bounty of 500 pounds, he would use 400 pounds annually for the construction of roads, bridges, and ferries. He would attempt, through the constructive improvement of his area, to establish communication with the Province of Georgia, West Florida, and the southern part of East Florida. The remaining 100 pounds would be used as salaries for a clergyman and a schoolmaster who would accompany the first 500 Greeks.[65]

On April 16 of the same year The Lords of Trade submitted their report on behalf of Turnbull's petition. It was their opinion that a subsidy of 40 shillings per person be granted to Turnbull for the first 500 Greeks imported, children excepted. They felt that it would greatly encourage more speculation of this sort. They stated that the Doctor's type of speculation was definitely for the good of the royal service. This subsidy was to be paid by Governor Grant through proper bills drawn upon the agent for the amount indicated. They stated that the subsidy for the two previous years and the current year was presently in the hands of the agent. The total amount on hand was 1100 pounds and this amount remained unappropriated at this time. The subsidy of 40 shillings per person would equal 1000 pounds and would leave a balance of 100 pounds in the agent's hands. The Lords of Trade recommended that this balance be used as a salary for the first Greek priest to arrive with the colony. The Lords were not enthusiastic about Turnbull's idea of making roads, ferries and bridges. They were not even sure that Parliament would continue to appropriate 500 pounds per annum as a subsidy.[66] They also recommended to George III that Doctor Turnbull be appointed to His Majesty's Council by the Governor of the Province in January while he was in East Florida. Crown approval was necessary, however, and the Lords of Trade recommended that he be given it.

The President of the Board of Trade notified Governor Grant of the Crown's decision to give Dr. Turnbull a subsidy of 40 shillings per person.[67] This subsidy was to be given for the first 500 Greeks to arrive in the Province, and only the first 500. In his communication to Governor Grant the Earl of Shelburne enclosed a copy of Dr. Turnbull's petition and the report and recommendations of the Board of Trade. The petition and report were included in order that the governor would have his administrative instructions for the actual payment of the 1,100-pound subsidy. The Earl of Shelburne instructed the governor to "give these settlers when they arrive every suitable encouragement."[68]

In the Province of East Florida, in the meantime, the Doctor's family was adding to the colony's acreage at the Mosquettos. Mary, Jane and Margaret, were each granted 5,000 acres.[69] The total acreage granted for the colony at the Mosquettos was now 80,000 acres. Of this total 20,000 acres were granted to Sir William Duncan; 20,000 acres granted to Commander Richard Temple on behalf of Lord Grenville, and 40,000 acres were granted to the Turnbull's. Most of the actual site of the colony may be identified as follows:

20,000 acres	on the Hillsborough River[70]
10,000 acres	on south side of fork of Nassau River
5,000 acres	on east side of Lake George
5,000 acres	on front fork of the Nassau River
5,000 acres	on the east side of Lake George
5,000 acres	lying across the lands of the middle branches of the Nassau River
3,600 acres	on Sugar Island
1,300 acres	on Spruce Creek
1,000 acres	60 miles south of St. Augustine
1,000 acres	on Don Pablo's Creek
250 acres	on west side of Tomoka Creek
200 acres	on Hillsborough River
200 acres	on Island Swamp east of Stockade Fort
200 acres	opposite an Island on Tomoka Creek

200 acres	on west side of Tomoka Creek
100 acres	75 miles south of St. Augustine
100 acres	on east side of Hillsborough River
50 acres	between Halifax River and Sea Beach north of Mosquito Inlet
1 lot	in city of New Smyrna south of Convent Lane

During the months of April, May, and June, Doctor Turnbull purchased seeds, tools and implements for the colony in East Florida. As yet he had no settlers, but he was preparing for the complicated logistical problem involved in shipping them across the Atlantic Ocean once he found them. He hired an agent, Mr. Edward Purnel, to represent him in the various parts of Europe and the Levant. And so in June 1767, the Doctor was prepared to leave England and find settlers for the colony he desired to establish at New Smyrna in His Majesty's Province of East Florida.[71]

III.

The Gathering of the Settlers

Doctor Turnbull sailed from England in search of colonists for his New Smyrna settlement in June 1767. He originally planned to begin his settlement with 500 Greeks skilled in the production of cotton and silk. But, while he was in England, Turnbull learned that he might be able to procure some settlers at Leghorn, Italy, and in southern France. The prospects of procuring some settlers of Leghorn seemed good. He decided to alter his plans and, while he was still in England, began preliminary negotiations to procure settlers from Leghorn And so, Leghorn was his first port of call instead of Greece. He arrived there some time in June.[72]

His first action on arrival was to contact the governor of Leghorn and obtain his approval for Italians to join this English colonial enterprise. The governor did state, however, that he would not approve of the exportation of Genoese silk manufacturers. Turnbull agreed to the Italian governor's decision, and sought potential colonists from a large group of unemployed Italians awaiting deportation from Italy. He was able to contact 110 of these people within a short period of time.[73]

The agreement that Turnbull made with the Italians was: (1) that he would pay their transportation costs to the Province of East Florida; (2) that he would provide for their care and well being in transit; (3) the Italians would be indebted to the colony for a period of seven or eight years; (4) at the end of their indebtedness, they were to be given 50 acres of land each, and a bonus of an additional five acres for each child in their family: (5) they were given the right to return to their own country at the end of a six-month period if they were dissatisfied with the land in East Florida.[74] Thus, the colony became a reality, and no longer an idea.

Turnbull's procurement of the Italians was not without difficulty, however, for even though an agreement with the Italian governor had been reached the latter caused Turnbull much consternation. When the actual movement of the Italians from their country began the governor did everything in his power to halt their further movement, and even sent threatening messages to them. It was only after requesting the British Consul in Leghorn to intercede for him that Turnbull was able to take his colonists out of Italy. But before he left Turnbull made arrangements to take out more Italians from Leghorn in October. He left his agent, Edward Pumel, to make the logistical arrangements. He gave Mr. Pumel instructions to procure a shipload of Italian settlers and transport them to Mahon, Minorca, in October.[75]

Turnbull's vessel, with 110 Italians on board, left Leghorn in early July 1767. Within a few days it entered the deep-water port of Mahon and the colonists were disembarked. Turnbull decided to leave the Italians in Mahon and use that port as a base of operations for further expansion of his colony. He planned to procure settlers and bring them to Mahon. He established a collecting point and assembly area for his colonists there. In so doing he simplified his logistical problem by having all his colonists in one central location. It was less expensive to procure settlers and bring them to a central location than to ship them all over the Mediterranean, where transportation costs remained high.[76]

With his first settlers safely placed and cared for in Minorca, Dr. Turnbull concentrated on preparations for continuing his quest for colonists. On July 11, 1767, he left Mahon bound for Greece.[77] This was to be his main effort, for the Greeks were his desire. He anticipated the procurement of 500 Greeks with little or no effort on his part. His expectations were soon to disappear through the efforts of organized business and a foreign government working hand in hand. The Levant Company, an English trading firm chartered during the reign of Elizabeth I, had agents placed in strategic positions in the Levant. The Company became fearful of Turnbull's plans in the Levant, and even more fearful of coming into direct conflict with him. Since the Levant Company was an English agency, and Turnbull an English subject, open conflict was not the best policy. The company solved its problem with Turnbull by notifying the Turkish authorities that he intended to remove useful subjects and transport them to the English Province of East Florida.[78]

The thought of losing subjects of the Ottoman Empire was more than the Turks could bear. Everywhere that Turnbull went the Turkish authorities appeared on the scene and prohibited him from recruiting settlers.[79] Turnbull wandered the Aegean aimlessly for weeks with little apparent success. On September 24, he wrote a letter to Governor Grant from the Island of Melo. He stated that he was proceeding to a port on the Peloponnesus to embark some Greeks.[80] He then went to Mani and to the port of Coron. The oppression of the Turks and the fear of being taken into slavery caused many people of this place to join Turnbull's colony.[81]

Turnbull left the port of Coron with his Greek settlers. From Coron he sailed to the islands of Crete, Santorin, and Smyrna.[82] In January, 1768, Turnbull left Greece and sailed for the port of Mahon, Minorca. He arrived there on February 3.[83] Three ships comprised his convoy from Greece. One ship arrived before his own, and another was expected to arrive carrying 200 Greeks aboard.[84]

Doctor Turnbull's colony was comprised of so many people of different languages that an international settlement actually evolved from his travels and selection. The colony in February consisted of 110 Italians from Leghorn, who married many young Minorcan women. These marriages increased the colony, and were encouraged by Turnbull.[85] There were an undetermined number of Greeks brought to Minorca by Turnbull himself. Mr. Pumel also brought an undetermined number of people from Leghorn in October 1767. The vessel sent by Pumel brought Corsicans and Italians from other parts of Italy.[86] There were a few Greeks from the island of Corsica aboard Pumel's vessel.[87] The Minorcans themselves began to join the colony, and these people eventually outnumbered the other linguistic groups of settlers.

The only known contract to exist between Turnbull and his settlers was the contract he made with the Minorcans. These people obligated themselves, of their own free will, to Mr. Andrew Turnbull as follows:

(1)   That Doctor Turnbull would be obligated to transport them to East Florida at his own expense.[88]

(2)   That upon arrival, those who wished to work at farming would be given the necessities of life. They would be provided for and maintained by Turnbull until "the productive lands are delivered to them"

(3)   The Minorcans themselves would judge the amount of land they were capable of cultivating, and they would be assigned to only that much land.

(4)   When their land initially produced, payments in produce would be given to Turnbull to reimburse him the amount he had spent on their well-being. After this payment, the settlers would be allowed to keep a sufficient amount of their produce for their own sustenance. The expenses involved in their transport to East Florida were not to be included in their indebtedness.

(5)   After the first harvest, Turnbull was to be given one-half of the land's produce. The remainder, after deducting the amount they would need for their maintenance, would be given to Turnbull in further payment of their indebtedness.

(6)   The term of the contract was to be for ten consecutive years. The term would begin at the first harvest of crops.

(7)   Neither Turnbull nor the contractors could separate themselves from this contract until the full term of the contract had expired.

(8)   The contractors were obligated to plant and cultivate only the kind of crops Turnbull desired.

(9)   The present and future possessions of all contractors were obligated to Turnbull during the full term of their contract.

(10)   Upon termination of the contract, each head of a family would receive 100 English quarters of land for himself. An additional 50 quarters would be given to each person in the family, male or female. This land would be their property forever, and would be given to them in the form of a "royal grant." 160 quarters of land is defined as having a perimeter of two English miles.

The total number of colonists at Turnbull's assembly area in Mahon in February 1768 is unknown. There are no existing records to indicate the number, and any effort to state a figure would be conjecture. It is known, however, that the majority of the colonists were Minorcans.[89] Their number increased daily through marriage and enlistment. In order to live in this assembly area, it was necessary to speak Greek, Italian, Catalan, and dialects of all three; otherwise it was necessary to remain with one's own linguistic group, which the majority must have done. Language must have been quite a problem at Turnbull's assembly area in Mahon.

According to the Proclamation of October, a petitioner had to settle a township grant with "the proper number of Protestant families." The Italian, Minorcan, and Corsican element of Turnbull's colony were undoubtedly Roman Catholic; the Greeks were undoubtedly Orthodox Catholics. Just how many Protestant families there were in the colony is not known, though it can be assumed that Protestants were definitely in the minority. To provide for the spiritual well being of the Roman Catholics, two Minorcan priests, Fathers Pedro Camps and Bartolome Casanovas, joined the colony.[90] A Greek priest was authorized to join the colony after the settlers arrived at New Smyrna, but as yet there was no priest to attend the Greeks.[91]

In 1768, Minorca was a British possession and the island of Mallorca Spanish. Minorca, according to the administrative system of the Roman Catholic Church, consisted of parishes within the diocese of Mallorca. The diocese was administered by a bishop whose cathedral was, of course, on the island of Mallorca. Contrary to the Treaty of Utrecht, 1713, exercise of religious freedom was not permitted on the British island of Minorca. The prelate was not permitted to administer his Minorcan parishes, for no ecclesiastical communication existed between Mallorca and Minorca; consequently, Fathers Camps and Casanovas never received permission to join the colony from their prelate.[92] This was a most awkward situation for Roman Catholic priests.

The question of ecclesiastical jurisdiction had to be answered before the colony sailed for East Florida. Florida was an English possession, and England was Protestant. Since no communication existed with their prelate, the priests appealed directly to the Holy See to answer this question. The answer they received instructed them to contact their new bishop in America. The Holy See evidently had failed to keep informed of the international situation, for no Roman Catholic bishop resided in English America. Fathers Camps and Casanovas were appointed apostolic missionaries, and both were extended wide privileges in their work. Father Camps was appointed pastor of the settlement, and Father Casanovas his assistant.[93]

Meanwhile, Dr. Turnbull was preparing for the transportation of his colony, and purchasing cuttings for grapes, olives and mulberries. He also purchased seeds, agricultural equipment, and silk worms.[94] All the cuttings, seeds and silkworm eggs had to be processed for shipment. Plants required water, and the eighteenth-century vessels carried only a limited supply To solve the problems of shipping plants, most planters shipped only seeds, and these were prepared for shipment in a very special way. All roots, vines and suckers were packed in a strong, iron-clasped cask, and filled with oil. Seeds were put in bottles filled with oil. The silkworm eggs were prepared in the same manner as seeds.[95]

By February, the colony had increased to almost one thousand men, women, and children. Instead of the 500 Greeks Turnbull sought he had almost twice that number, and the colony continued to increase daily. More ships, laden with colonists, had arrived at Mahon.[96] The increase in settlers required additional financial aid, and required logistics never before attempted. No one before Turnbull had ever attempted to bring so large a number of people, in one trip, to colonize an area in North America. Andrew Turnbull was prepared to risk everything he and his partners had.

In one respect Turnbull had to risk failure. He and his partners had been granted about 80,000 acres of land at the Mosquettos in East Florida. Turnbull and his partners wanted more land than they were actually granted, and this had to be considered by them; also to be considered, was the stipulation with which the land had been granted to them. Under the English government's terms, the land had to be settled with one person for every 100 acres within three years, or Turnbull and his partners would forfeit one-third of their grant. The amount of land at the Mosquettos would require 800 people to satisfy the land occupation requirement of the English government. If more land was acquired, more settlers would be required in proportion. Turnbull also had to consider the possibility of losing settlers in transit and after arriving. Many things can happen to a human being, and human beings were his investment. It would be extremely difficult and expensive for him to supply a ship in East Florida and search for more settlers. His finances were not healthy at this time. There was the subsidy he had been awarded by the English government to consider also. The more settlers he placed ashore at East Florida, the greater the subsidy.

By March 28, Dr. Turnbull was prepared to depart from the island of Minorca. As a final arrangement he contacted British naval officials, and arranged for a naval escort to protect his convoy from nations at war with the Barbary States.[97] Captain Vanput, commanding His Majesty's Frigate *Caryefort*, agreed to escort the convoy as far as Gilbraltar. Turnbull was required to contact Commodore Spry at Gibraltar to arrange further escort from Gibraltar to the Madeiras Islands.[98]

Sometime between March 28 and April 3, 1768, Dr. Turnbull embarked his settlers on six vessels and left Minorca. On April 4, the convoy was at Gibraltar, and Turnbull discovered there that many stowaways were aboard the ships. The colony continued to grow, even at sea. In addition to the stowaways, five births were recorded. The Doctor found that his ships were carrying 1,400 passengers, and that they were overcrowded. To alleviate this overcrowded condition, Turnbull hired a large Dutch vessel. He was later informed by the British Navy that the Dutch vessel could not enter American waters, and so was forced to look elsewhere for transportation. In lieu of the Dutch vessel, he contracted for two smaller English ships to carry his settlers.[99]

Turnbull's convoy now consisted of eight vessels carrying 1,400 passengers. All of his settlers were healthy and none were deformed or maimed.[100] His loading plan for the eight vessels was *Charming Betsy*, 232 passengers; *Henry and Carolina*, 142 passengers; *Elizabeth*, 190 passengers; *Friendship*, 198 passengers; *New Fortune*, 226 passengers; *Hope*, 150 passengers; *American Soldier*, 145 passengers; *Betsey*, 120 passengers. This made a total of 1,403 men, women, and children.[101]

Turnbull contacted Commodore Spry on his arrival at Gibraltar for further convoy protection. The Commodore ordered Captain Vanput to continue his convoy protection mission with the *Caryefort* as far as the Madeiras Islands.[102] After making these, and other arrangements, Turnbull and his convoy sailed from the island of Gibraltar on April 17, 1768. This time the convoy's destination was St. Augustine, British East Florida.[103]

IV.

The Settlement of
New Smyrna

Preparations for the arrival of the colony at the Mosquettos had begun before Turnbull's return to England from East Florida. Now, while the colony was at sea, preparations were continuing at St. Augustine and at the Mosquettos. Mr. Osborne, an English gentleman who owned an estate near the colony site, had offered his estate and Negro slaves to aid Turnbull on his arrival with the colony. Some huts were under construction at the colony site. A few huts had already been constructed, enough, perhaps, for 500 settlers. Governor Grant had already laid out plans for assistance when the colony arrived. He planned to send his provisional schooner and other vessels to Mosquetto Inlet to assist in disembarking the colonists. The governor also planned to send the colonists directly to Mosquetto Inlet by ship instead of disembarking them at St. Augustine.[104] The entire province of East Florida was equally anticipating the arrival of Turnbull's colony. News of Turnbull's success in procuring settlers had been spread throughout the province. [105]

The first four vessels of Turnbull's convoy reached St. Augustine on June 26, 1768.[106] These ships brought almost 700 colonists. The remaining four ships with the rest of the settlers aboard were blown off course by the trade winds, but they arrived before August 10. The delay in arrival of these last four vessels caused some alarm in the province, for death had already reached Turnbull's colonists. [107] Of the 1,403 colonists who sailed from Gibraltar, only 1,255 arrived safely in East Florida.[108] On one ship alone, 48 settlers were said to have died.[109] Misfortune again came to the colony in the form of death. A ship bringing 500 Negro slaves directly from Africa was wrecked on the southern coast of Florida, and all aboard were lost.[110] The Negro slaves were purchased to do the heavier work of the colony, for most land needed to be cleared at the Mosquettos.[111] This came as bad news for the colonists, for they would be required, in addition to establishing the plantations, to clear all the land themselves.

Nevertheless, many other difficulties arose through failure to continue with plans made prior to the settlers' arrival in St. Augustine. Instead of disembarking all the settlers at the Mosquettos as planned, part of them were moved by land and part by ship.[112] At any rate, by August 10, the colonists had been moved to New Smyrna and placed on plantations.[113] This was undoubtedly done by placing each language group separate from the others; all the Minorcans together, the Greeks together and the Italians. One thing is certain, all the families were kept together.[114] Even the governor considered that the different languages spoken at New Smyrna would aid in keeping the colony from leaving both New Smyrna and Turnbull.[115] English was the language mainly spoken in Florida, and not many colonists knew it.[116]

The settlers were, however, under direct governmental control of the English government. Under terms of their contract, they were indebted to Turnbull. For control purposes, they were organized into plantations by language groups and families. These families and groups of families were placed under the jurisdiction of an overseer, often one of their own number.[117] The overseer supervised the group's work according to the directions of Turnbull or his principal overseer, Mr. Cutter.[118] Under this organization the settlers began to work in earnest. They began to clear the land and build some type of shelter for both themselves and their crops.[119] Shelter was a necessity for these people, for many of them became ill. Scurvy, a disease that often struck in eighteenth-century sea voyages was with them yet.[120] A large number of settlers were plagued with this dread disease, and many died from gangrene of the mouth because of scurvy.[121] These people were in a hurry to get the land cleared and crops harvested, for they were hungry. In the first place, there was no surplus of food crops in East Florida because the province was young and unpopulated. The crops that were grown were undoubtedly enough for the plantation on which they were grown, and no more crops were grown other than "money crops." Governor Grant did have the foresight to place four months' supply of provision at the Mosquettos for the colony's sustenance.[122] The colonists would starve after that period if they did not grow their own crops. To alleviate any future disaster which might befall the colony through lack of funds, Governor Grant displayed initiative by asking for royal assistance as early as July 2, six days after the colony arrived at his province.[123] These funds would be needed to buy provisions in the event of crop failure before their colony's first harvest.

Under the conditions of hunger and discontent, violence came to the colony two months after it arrived in New Smyrna. Life went on as usual in the colony on August 18. Dr. Turnbull had left New Smyrna with some gentlemen from Carolina who had visited the colony site. These gentlemen were much impressed with the progress the colony had made in such a brief space of time. They stated that it was undoubtedly the best colony in America.[124]

The next day, at eleven o'clock in the morning, Carlo Forni, one of the overseers, declared himself the chief spokesman for the Greek and Italian elements of the colony, and a riot ensued. The disorder began with 20 individuals and soon increased to almost 300. In the confusion that followed, Carlo Forni and his followers seized the storehouse. They looted the rum, wine, oil, limes, blankets, and flour. They captured the principal overseer, Mr. Cutter, and later wounded him. Someone cut off one of his ears and two of his fingers.[125] Then the rum was freely handed out by Forni, and confusion reigned. A plan of escape was put forward by Forni and he issued a death warning to all who would not accompany him to Havana. With escape in mind, he seized Turnbull's sloop and another vessel, and provisioned with looted supplies. Forni and his followers decided that the entire colony should rise up in revolt; but they would not, the majority of the settlers were fearful of this drunken madness. The entire Minorcan element resisted Forni's pleas and later demands. For this they were looted and plundered just as the storehouse and vessels had been.[126]

Meanwhile, two Italians escaped the mob and ran to the main plantation house, about four miles from the riot scene. They told the overseer there about the events, and exaggerated the entire morning's happenings. The overseer immediately dispatched a notice to Turnbull, adding to the exaggeration of his two Italian informers. The dispatch reached Turnbull at midnight August 19, at a place called Mount Oswald. He was very much alarmed and immediately sent a dispatch to Governor Grant. He informed Grant of what had happened and begged for the governor to come to his aid. He further informed the governor that he was returning to New Smyrna at once. Governor Grant received Turnbull's dispatch on August 20 at eight o'clock in the evening, and lost no time in making preparations for the capture of the instigators of the riot. At five o'clock in the morning of August 21, H.M.S. *East Florida* and another vessel left St. Augustine bound for Mosquetto Inlet. The ships were loaded with troops of the Ninth Regiment, provisions, and ammunition. At the same time Major Whitmore, Ninth Regimental Commander in St. Augustine, sent a troop unit by land. The troop unit could not have prevented the rioters' escape, for the roads were too bad and the distance to the Mosquettos was too great.[127]

On the morning of August 22, at eleven o'clock the *East Florida* encountered its objective, the stolen vessel. It was still in Mosquetto harbor awaiting a proper tide to cross the bar. The rioters were still aboard, about 300 in number. On seeing the *East Florida* approach the harbor, a gun crew aboard the stolen vessel went into action. One round was fired at the *East Florida*, and the counter-recoil of the weapon caused the stolen vessel to run aground on a bar in the harbor. The rioters were taken ashore and placed in custody. Carlo Forni and five others were taken to St. Augustine as prisoners of the governor.[128]

Not all of the mutineers were aboard the vessel in Mosquetto inlet harbor. About 20 or 30 escaped and made their way as far south as the Keys. They too were captured by an English vessel from Providence, and taken to St. Augustine. All the mutineers were captured and made prisoners of the governor.[129]

The mutineers were given trial by jury. Most of them were acquitted for lack of evidence. All but five were finally released. Carlo Forni and Guiseppi Massadoti, alias Bresiano, who wounded Mr. Cutter, were condemned to death by hanging.[130] Georgi Stephanopoli was found guilty of felony for taking forcibly and carrying away a boat belonging to Sir Charles Burdet, Baronet. Clotha Corona was found guilty of felony for breaking into Dr. Turnbull's warehouse and stealing limes, blankets, and flour. Elia Medi was found guilty of felony for stealing a boat belonging to Dr. Turnbull.[131]

Governor Grant reprieved Stephanopoli, Corona, and Medi, and set them at liberty "till His Majesty's pleasure was known."[132] One of the reprieved men was ordered to be executioner of Forni and Massodoti. Bernard Romans, who had served on the jury witnessed the execution. Mr. Romans stated:

> *On this occasion I saw one of the most moving scenes I ever experienced; long and obstinate was the struggle of this man's mind, who repeatedly called out, that he chose to die rather than be the executioner of his friends in distress; this not a little perplexed Mr. Woolridge, the sheriff, till at length the entreaties of the victims themselves, put an end to the conflict in his breast, by encouraging him to the act. Now we beheld a man thus compelled to mount the ladder, take leave of his friends in the most moving manner, kissing them a moment before he committed them to ignominious death.[133]*

On November 2, 1769, Governor Grant was informed by the Secretary of State, Lord Hillsborough, that George III had granted a full pardon to Stephanopoli, Corona, and Medi. Governor Grant had the power to do so but he did not.[134]

Thus peace was restored at New Smyrna. The trial of the mutineers and the execution of Forni and Massadoti eased the mind of Governor Grant and his

Council. They felt that fear of the gallows would ward off any further attempt at revolt. Turnbull stated that his losses resulting from the uprising amounted to four or five hundred pounds, and that he lost 35 troublesome settlers.[135]

The uprising at New Smyrna caused the governor of the province to face events he thought would never happen. He had never considered the possibility of trouble with the settlers at New Smyrna. He was now concerned with the possibility of further difficulties with Indians of the province. The Indians hated the Spaniards, and the governor feared the Indians would think that the colonists were Spaniards. The planters in the neighborhood of the settlement at New Smyrna were also alarmed at the possibilities of more riots. One planter, Dr. Stork, near the spot when the insurrection happened, died of fright.[136] With the fear of future uprisings and trouble with the Indians of the province in mind, the governor asked the Board of Trade to approve the construction of a stockade at the Mosquettos. This had been approved earlier for the colony that was to have been established by Mr. John Savage and his Bermudians. Governor Grant also asked that the Board of Trade approve the construction of a port of entry to be built at Mosquetto inlet. He further requested that a permanent garrison of 100 troops be stationed at New Smyrna.[137]

V.

New Smyrna's Economic Development

Life at the colony, after the uprising, settled down to hard work. Hunger still prevailed at New Smyrna, and gangrene continued to take a heavy toll of lives. By the end of 1768, 300 men and women and 150 children died from scurvy and hunger.[138]

The foods on which the colony depended were mainly hominy grits, fish, shellfish, and oysters, and oysters were plentiful in the Mosquetto lagoon only during the winter months.[139] There was little that the settlers could do to sustain themselves. The land had not been completely cleared for planting, for a considerable amount of time was necessary to clear and prepare the 80,000 acres at New Smyrna for planting. The provincial governor stated that it would require a minimum of two years before the colony would obtain relief from the hunger suffered through lack of crops.[140] The provincial government continued to express concern about the starving condition of the colony.

The settlers, nevertheless, continued to prepare the land and to unpack the seeds and plants they had brought with them.[141] The preparation of the seeds for planting was a tedious task. The wooden casks were drained of the oil they contained, and the oil was put in an empty vessel suited for storage. The oil was to be used later for other purposes. The seeds and plants were wiped dry of oil, and were rubbed with dry ashes until the ashes came off dry. The empty wooden casks were sawed in half and used to make tubs, buckets and pails. Some were left whole, and used for storing various liquids. A great deal of care was given to the silkworm eggs. After being removed from the container of oil, they were mixed with dry ashes and moved about, very carefully, on a piece of blotting paper to remove all the oil and ashes. This process was continued with fresh ashes and blotting paper until no trace of oil remained in the ashes or on the blotting paper.[142]

Some huts had been constructed before the arrival of the colony, but many more were needed. Many settlers labored building shelters for themselves, constructed from palmetto logs. The spacious church of San Pedro was built at New Smyrna for the Roman Catholic element, and a brick residence was constructed for the two Catholic priests.[143] The family lived in a separate hut, or temporary shelter, until better accommodations were made available. The unmarried members of the colony lived in three separate huts.[144] Little is known about the types and sizes of the buildings at the settlement and their number is also unknown. The settlers were obliged to live in small, hastily constructed huts until the colony was disbanded. There were not the necessary tools and materials to build true houses, with the exception of the main plantation house, in which Dr. Turnbull and his family lived.[145]

Government assistance was required to prevent the entire colony from starving, and Governor Grant began to ask for governmental aid almost as soon at the colonist reached East Florida soil. It was almost certain that Sir William Duncan and Lord Greenville would not offer more money to the enterprise without seeing something substantial in the way of monetary progress.[146] There was only starvation at the colony, and progress revolved around the growth of the meager crops that were planted. There was land yet to clear and plant, and more seeds were expected from England.[147] Meanwhile, the colonists were living on a meager diet of fish and hominy grits. Their provisions at the best of times were only a quart of corn per day, and two ounces of salted pork per week. Fish abounded in the Mosquetto lagoon, but settlers were denied the liberty of fishing as often as they pleased. Instead of allowing each family to do with its meager fare as it wanted, it was forced to join others in a common mess. All would come to one common copper kettle at the beat of a drum. This kettle contained the meager ration of hominy grits.[148]

In December, 1768, the situation at New Smyrna seemed grave. Governor Grant "cried for their poor hungry souls," and feared, at the same time, that the disaster of the entire colony starving would ruin the possibilities of populating the infant province of East Florida.[149]

By September, 1769, the colony had formed into a group of farms extending along the river front. Each farm was placed 210 feet from the next. The plot of each farmland was 210 feet wide at the front, 210 feet at the back and was many acres deep. The physical layout of the farms of the settlement, and the proximity of one farm to the other, gave New Smyrna the appearance of a Chinese plantation. It was in the early formation of the settlement that indigo was first planted and stressed as a cash crop. There were other crops planted at this time such as grape vines, olives, and mulberry trees. The grapes would be used in making wine, the olives for oil they contained, and the mulberry trees for silkworm culture. The principal aim of the colony was to make money for its investors, but the primary concern at this time was to grow enough food crops to keep the colonists from starving to death.[150]

By March, 1769, most of the colonists had regained their health and strength. The Minorcans had cleared seven miles of river front property and planted gardens of food crops. They worked in their gardens cheerfully and nursed the tender crops with great care. The governor was still uneasy about the state of the colony in regards to its sustenance, and he constantly reminded Turnbull to keep at least four months' supply of provisions on hand at all times. Turnbull was still hard pressed for provisions, for none of his supplies had arrived at New Smyrna on time. There was only one month's supply of corn on hand at the Mosquettos. To alleviate this problem, Governor Grant privately sent the *East Florida* to Charleston. He gave private instructions to his agent in that settlement to load the schooner with corn. The governor gave the ship's captain secret instructions to proceed directly to New Smyrna with his load of corn. To disguise the purpose of sending the *East Florida* on this secret mission, Governor Grant told his administrative subordinates that the vessel was being sent to Savannah to procure lumber and other supplies needed for the province.[151]

In this month financial relief also came to New Smyrna. Mr. Thomas Bradshaw, the Provincial Treasurer, presented an affidavit to the effect that he had been directed by the Earl of Hillsborough to pay from royal funds the sum of 2,000 pounds to the governor of East Florida. The sum was to be used by the governor for the assistance of the settlement of New Smyrna.[152] Further instructions from Lord Hillsborough, the Secretary of State for Colonial Affairs, to Governor Grant was that the 2,000 pounds was given to him to be used as an emergency fund. The governor was instructed to use this money at any time he felt it necessary to do so. He was also instructed to negotiate with Dr. Turnbull, and then to purchase whatever was thought best. The governor was to specify the source of supplies and accompany his draft with proper vouchers and accounts.[153] Lord Hillsborough was concerned with Governor Grant's interest in the settlement at New Smyrna. His Lordship continued to state in his correspondence that he was always "trusting that you [Grant] will not undertake any service which shall induce an expense to the public beyond the grants of Parliament."[154]

This emergency fund for the colony came as timely news to Governor Grant. In his correspondence to Lord Hillsborough the governor stated that he would not spend the entire fund until the situation at New Smyrna became worse. In defense of Turnbull's desire to keep such a large colony, the governor stated that Turnbull was hurried into accepting all the Minorcans because they were starving on Minorca. The colony had already cost Turnbull and his associates in London more than 20,000 pounds and the associates would no longer assist monetarily. The governor was still concerned with the fact that Turnbull's settlement would collapse from starvation. He was sure that they would raise crops to provide for their sustenance if they were given a few vital necessities. Clothing was the major item needed, and when the emergency fund was used it would be only for the bare minimum to keep the colony going. The items of purchase would most probably consist of Indian corn, salt, and cloth to make garments. With the idea of no monetary assistance from Turnbull's associates, the governor again begged for continuation of the bounty of 500 pounds annually given Turnbull on his arrival.[155]

Eighteen months had passed since Governor Grant was notified that an emergency fund of 2,000 pounds had been placed in the hands of the Provincial Treasurer, and the fund remained unspent. Governor Grant was obviously not as concerned with the possibility that the colony would starve itself out of existence as he was with the fear of spending the funds incorrectly. He was a government official, and as such was required to conduct his office with a certain amount of restraint. The funds, after all, were from the people of Great Britain. Turnbull was undoubtedly anxious to get his hands on goods that the money would buy. The colonists themselves were interested in food, clothing, shelter, and a few comforts to make life worthwhile for them.

In September, 1770, the entire subsidy of 1769 had been spent by Turnbull on emergency rations for the colony. This actually saved the settlement from starvation.[156] A total of 155 men and women and 22 children died at the settlement in 1769.[157] The settlers were now in much better health and their morale, for all practical purposes, was good. A great deal more of the land had been cleared, and a consumable amount of Indian corn, peas, potatoes, and greens of all kinds were harvested. The production of indigo was going well, and the produce was soon to be shipped to England. This shipment of indigo was to be the settlement's first export.[158]

The settlers were still destitute, and they had no conveniences. They were ill clothed, and many of them were almost naked. They were living in the small palmetto log nuts they found or hastily built. Dr. Turnbull did not have the money nor the credit to buy cloth for them to make clothing. There was still a lack of tools and materials to build houses. In order to obtain any item they needed to clothe themselves, the colonists continued to look for royal assistance.[159]

The governor was still asking for continuation of the subsidy to Turnbull, and in the year 1770, Governor Grant at last decided to spend the emergency fund. He submitted a requisition for 1,000 pounds' worth of material for the colony.

He requisitioned:

3000 yds.	Best blue plains
500 yds.	Best white plains
3000 yds	Checkered linens
2000 yds	Stript linens
500 yds	Stript cottons
4000 yds	Scots Osnabrugs
600	Negro blankets
600 prs.	Men's shoes of different sizes
60 doz.	Indigo Sickles
60 doz.	Bread hoes, Crowley's, of a meddling size
	Building nails, the greatest part 6-penny[160]

Governor Grant submitted this requisition on behalf of Dr. Turnbull who had pressed him to transmit the requisition for Lord Hillsborough's consideration. A formal request was then made for the continuation of the subsidy for the year 1770. Plans for the purchase of the requested items were laid before his Lordship. Mr. Dixon, Turnbull's agent in London, was to procure the 1,000 pounds necessary for payment of the items requisitioned directly from the Treasury in London, and purchase the items requested. Mr. Dixon was to pack these supplies and ship them to Charleston, if no vessel could be found going directly to St. Augustine. The remaining 1,000 pounds of the emergency fund would be used to support further the settlement in the manner seen most suitable to the governor.[16]

A considerable amount of food, materials, tools and implements was shipped for use in New Smyrna before and after the arrival of the settlers. On December 23, 1767, six months before the colonists set foot on Florida soil, the sloop *Wanchy*, with Samuel Case as its master, sailed from Savannah with 2,100 bushels of Indian corn in her hold.

The Minorcans had been at their new home slightly more than a year when the schooner *East Florida*, commanded by James Wallace, left Charleston. She sailed on August 1, 1769, and her hatches protected 400 bushels of corn and a large copper still. Thirty days later a large cargo was shipped from Charleston on the schooner *Carson*, captained by Charles Smyth. These items were:

100	M 4-penny nails
80	M 6-penny nails
80	M 10-penny nails
20	M 20-penny nails
156	falling hoes
170	grubbing hoes
	Several dozen Philadelphia hoes
300	barrels of salt
200	iron pots
4	ship saw files
30	yards white plains

In addition, the *Carson* carried 800 bushes of Indian corn. Unfortunately she was forced to put in at Savannah on account of bad weather.

In 1770 food was the main shipment to New Smyrna. When the schooner *Live Oak* departed from Savannah on July 17 under Nathaniel Porter it carried 2,100 bushels of Indian corn. On the same day the schooner *Sally* put out of Charleston. Her cargo manifest listed 454 bushels of red peas, 332 ½ bushels of black-eyed peas, 90 bushels of peas, and 20 barrels of rice. The schooner *Active* left Charleston on November 10, and its hold was filled with 125 barrels of flour, 27 barrels of rice and 7 barrels of rum. The master of *Active* bore the same name of another famous master who had sailed many, many years before him, John Hawkins. Some shipments of food at dates unspecified in the manuscripts do not add or subtract from the significance of this narrative. They were of like nature.[162]

A continuation of the 2,000-pound subsidy, so often called for by Governor Grant for the New Smyrna settlement, was at last refused by the English government. The Secretary of State, Lord Hillsborough, felt that the subsidy should be continued, but he would not authorize any further expense to the public on account of the settlement of New Smyrna. He informed Governor Grant that the original 2,000-pound subsidy was an emergency fund only, and was given upon proper application of the governor of the province. This subsidy was by no means intended to encourage any expectation of a further sum. The Secretary of State referred all further requests for funds to the Lords of the Treasury. He placed the responsibility of granting additional funds for the colony on someone else.[163]

An official of the Board of Trade, Mr. Grey Cooper, transmitted to the Lords of the Treasury the copy of Governor Grant's request for a continuation of the royal subsidy.[164] This subsidy was requested by the governor to augment the annual bounty given to Turnbull and authorized by Parliament to encourage the culture of certain types of plants in East Florida.

The Lords of the Treasury rendered their decision in regards to this additional 2,000 pounds. After resuming consideration of the request for more money for New Smyrna, they stated in a letter written by Mr. John Robinson on their behalf:

> *I am directed by my Lords' Council of the Treasury to acquaint you for the information of the Earl of Hillsborough, that their Lordships having by minutes of the board of 23 March 1769 consented that Governor Grant should draw for a sum not succeeding 2,000 pounds for the support of the Greek Colonists at the same time desired it might be understood by Governor Grant that the public were to be at no further expense upon that account. Their Lordships do not think themselves authorized to allow any farther sum of money for this service.*[165]

Governor Grant was informed of the Lords of the Treasury decision. He had not given up hope for the continuation of the additional 2,000-pound subsidy, however, and continued to ask for it through the Secretary of State in London. He felt that he was not getting the full cooperation of the government in England, and that if Hillsborough would back up his request, the Treasury would support New Smyrna further.[166] This additional support never came, for the Lords of the Treasury had voiced their opinion, and they never wavered in it. It is not yet known if the 500-pound annual subsidy granted by Parliament in 1769 continued to be granted to Turnbull. Probably the colony had to suffer on its own. Monetary progress was its only salvation and by 1771 starvation at New Smyrna was not the main problem. Enough crops had been grown to sustain the settlement. The death rate had declined by 1770, for only 34 men and women, and 3 children died that year.[167]

New Smyrna's major problem in 1770 was to show monetary progress. Cash crops had to be grown and sold. Money was necessary to buy more materials and building supplies. This was Turnbull's problem now, and not the government's. In 1771 Governor Grant left the province of East Florida and the province was administered by the Lieutenant Governor, John Moultrie.[168] When Governor

Grant returned to England pleas from New Smyrna for governmental aid monetarily ended.

Communication between the Mosquettos and St. Augustine was extremely difficult. To alleviate the problem of communicating with the capital of the province, a good road was required. In 1770 Turnbull and other planters at the Mosquettos called upon Governor Grant to build a good road from St. Augustine to their plantations. In order to go to St. Augustine from New Smyrna it was necessary to travel by horse. Many of the planters had lost their horses on the difficult track to St. Augustine because of the terrible condition of the road. Governor Grant began to make repairs of the road by working on the worst parts first. He intended to begin construction of causeways and bridges over the swampy and marshy places in April. He promised to build a good road by degrees.[169]

In the latter part of April, 1771, a group of 72 Indians appeared at the place of Mr. Spalding, the principal trader in Latchway. The Upper Creek Chief, Cowkeeper, head spokesman for the group, pressed Mr. Spalding to give his braves blankets, shirts, paint, powder, and balls, an amount of goods that was valued at 30 pounds. They promised to pay later for these provisions, but if Spalding refused them, they would take his entire supply of rice amounting to 2 barrels. Cowkeeper stated that he and his people were hungry. Mr. Spalding was loath to give them what they demanded, but he could not deny them. The Indian braves were then divided into three groups by Cowkeeper. He headed one party himself, another was lead by Long Warrior, and the third by an unidentified Indian chief. Mr. Spalding began to question them concerning their plans, and he was told by Cowkeeper that he and the two other chiefs had received information that a settlement of Spaniards and Yamasee Indians had been built near the Mosquettos. They were going to find out if this information was true. If they did find a settlement of Spaniards and Yamasees there, they planned to attack it and burn the settlement to the ground.[170] En route to the Mosquettos, the war parties were informed that the settlement of Spaniards and Yamasees did in fact exist. They were told that it had been built on Cape Florida. Further information misrepresented Dr. Turnbull's colony at New Smyrna as a settlement of Spaniards, and this information brought the Indians to the Mosquettos.[171]

When they arrived at the Mosquettos they made camp near the cow pen of the Minorcan settlement. They were sulky, out of humor, hungry and they beat some of the Minorcan boat crew they found near the spot where they made camp. Meanwhile Dr. Turnbull was in St. Augustine. He received a report that a large body of Indians was near New Smyrna, and he returned at once to his settlement. On his arrival Turnbull approached the Indians near his cow pen, and was told by Cowkeeper of their purpose in that part of the country. Dr. Turnbull assured Cowkeeper that he had no Spaniards in his settlement and that there was no Yamasee settlement near New Smyrna. Then he invited Cowkeeper, Long Warrior and the other Indian chiefs with about twenty braves to his plantation house. He fed them and convinced them that the settlers at New Smyrna were not Spaniards. Doctor Turnbull's party put them in a better humor.[172]

Two days later the Indians broke camp at the cow pen and divided themselves into two parties. One party was led by Cowkeeper and the other by Long Warrior. Long Warrior's party left the Mosquettos the same day. Before his departure Turnbull gave Long Warrior a calf for his braves. His party returned to Latchaway via the head of the St. John's River. Cowkeeper's party was still intent on discovering the location of the Yamasse settlement. To assure the Creek chief of his good intentions, Dr Turnbull sent Langley Bryant and Black Sandy, both from his settlement, to accompany this war party, and to try to convince them that there was no Yamasee settlement. Before leaving he instructed Bryant and Black Sandy to remain with the Indians until they saw them pass the southern plantations on the Mosquetto River, but the Indians went no farther than Captain Bisset's plantation. Cowkeeper was convinced that he had been given incorrect information concerning a Yamasee camp being built in the area, and he returned to New Smyrna. The Indians were again fed and given much rum, and peace was restored to New Smyrna. Cowkeeper beat some his braves for offering to kill a calf belonging to the Minorcan settlement. As silently as they had appeared the Indians left. [173]

This incident with the Indians of the province gave rise to many uneasy days in New Smyrna. The settlers were afraid for their lives. An incident such as this had never happened before. Dr. Turnbull himself was uneasy. The only means of protecting the settlement was the detachment of the 31st Regiment, consisting of one sergeant and eight men. Dr. Turnbull requested a larger detachment of soldiers from the lieutenant governor. He reminded Governor Moultrie that the English government was obliged to protect him, his family, and his settlers.

On June 6, 1771, a council meeting was held in the governor's office in St. Augustine, and Turnbull appeared at this meeting. He presented to the governor and his council a written version of the Indian incident. He formally asked for more troops at New Smyrna. Turnbull told how terrified the settlers were at the thought that more Indians would some day return and kill them. The governor informed Turnbull that he was not in the least apprehensive of the Indians' intentions to commit any act of hostility. He was of the opinion that the king of England and the Indians of the province were on the best of terms, and that they would never be any major difficulty with the Indians. He was also of the opinion that it would be doing the settlement of New Smyrna a valuable service as far as morale was concerned to strengthen the detachment of the 31st Regiment. Additional troops there would command respect from any hunting parties or war parties passing that way, and would prevent irregularities that might otherwise happen. The additional troops would also tend to quiet the minds of the frightened settlers, and give them confidence in the government of East Florida. On the advice of Council, Governor Moultrie formally requested a strengthening of the detachment at New Smyrna from Major MacKenzie, Commander of Troops of the 31st Regiment in St. Augustine.[174]

Major MacKenzie informed the governor that same day that, in his opinion, the current detachment of the 31st Regiment presently there was sufficient. He reminded the governor that the troop's primary mission at New Smyrna was to prevent mutiny and insurrection among the Greek settlers. He told the governor that if any incident other than mutiny and insurrection happened at the settlement requiring more troops, a formal request would have to be made to General Gage, the Commander and Chief of the British Army in America.[175]

The rift between the governor of the province and the commander of troops was made known to Lord Hillsborough. He informed the governor, six months later, that he was of the opinion that Moultrie had acted wisely and properly in asking major MacKenzie for additional troops for New Smyrna. He further added that he would not fail, at the proper time, to consider what measures it would be advisable to take in consequence of the major's refusal to comply with the governor's request.[176]

By September, 1771, the part of the road from St. Augustine to the Mosquettos which Governor Grant had contracted for was completed. Governor Moultrie stated that the road was constructed in such a manner that it would not require any additional work or repairs for many years. The bridges were firm and made of substantial materials. The causeways were well made, and the road was well opened. Any number of carts or wagons could pass with ease in the worst kind of weather over 20 miles of good road toward the Mosquettos. But this was not quite half way to New Smyrna. The first waters of the Mosquetto River were more than 25 miles from the ground where the new road terminated. According to estimates it would require between 250 and 300 pounds to complete the project. This road was badly needed to ensure communications. It would be of great service to this part of the province if communication could be established with St. Augustine, whether by land or water. The entire produce of that part of the country might then be brought with safety and certainty to St. Augustine, which was not possible at the present time. Besides, vessels were still required to risk the dangers of the sea and the crossing of bars, and vessels were not available at all times, especially when they were most needed.[177]

To complete the road, Governor Moultrie called upon Lord Hillsborough for assistance in procuring the necessary capital. About 500 pounds would be needed to build a road from the first waters of the Mosquetto River to the river's inlet, New Smyrna. This was a distance of about 30 miles. After this last stretch was completed the entire road would be finished.[178]

Four months later Lord Hillsborough informed Governor Moultrie that he had taken cognizance of the request concerning the construction of the road. He stated that he would not fail to apprise the Lords of Trade of the necessity for the road when they considered the estimate of funds for East Florida for the next year.[179]

New Smyrna was on a more solid footing by 1771. Cash crops were being produced, and money was coming in from the sale of these crops. Business on the plantation at New Smyrna was so good that Turnbull resigned from his seat on the East Florida Council that year. His reason for resigning was that the settlement required all his time and efforts.[180] His enterprise was paying off.

In 1772 the Reverend Mr. Frasier, Protestant minister at the Mosquettos, died, and the settlements there were without a Protestant minister. To furnish the plantation with a Protestant minister the Reverend Mr. Forbes of St. Augustine was assigned an additional duty to go to the Mosquettos at regular intervals and conduct services. In order to reimburse Mr. Forbes for expenses he would incur traveling to and from the Mosquettos, Governor Moultrie gave him, in addition to his own salary, the salary that had been given Mr. Frasier.[181]

In 1772 New Smyrna numbered 175 families, approximately 500 people. Most of these people were Roman Catholics, parishioners of Father Camps. The majority was still Minorcan, though there were still Italian and Greek people, many of whom had intermarried by this time. The Roman Catholic religion was devoutly practiced in New Smyrna and the Church of San Pedro was the center of activity of the Minorcans and Italians there. The Church had been built much earlier, and was undoubtedly the first building completed. It was modestly adorned, and contained a high altar, a central figure of the Savior, a statue of the Prince of Apostles and a figure of St. Anthony. Christian doctrine was taught to the children of the settlement within its walls. Religious processions were held openly. The priests, Fathers

Camps and Casanovas, were very well respected, even by the English. Father Camps was even gratified by the fact that he could count as one of the faithful of the parish, Mrs. Turnbull herself.[182]

As for the produce of the colony, an abundance of sugar, cotton, rice and corn were shipped from the coquina wharfs of New Smyrna. Cochineal insects for making scarlet dye were exported. But, it was indigo which received the main attention. The cloth mills in England needed blue dye and indigo became a premium product.[183] East Florida was suitable for the production of indigo. The plant grew wild there, and it did not take long for Turnbull to realize that he should turn his attention to the production of this dye. Even Governor Grant was looking for an easier process to produce and export the dye. Dr. Turnbull spent many days at other indigo plantations in the province trying to improve his techniques of production of indigo at New Smyrna.[184]

Sometime in January, 1773, Governor Moultrie made an inspection of the southernmost plantations of East Florida, now extending to the first waters of the Indian River. A distance of over 100 miles south of St. Augustine. The governor found things going well there, especially at the plantation of Mr. Elliot; he was shown an experiment involving the amount of sugar that could be obtained from one acre of sugar cane. But unfortunately the sugar was still wet, and could not be weighed while he was there. As a result, he did not know the outcome of the experiment, though he was reasonably sure that a considerable amount of good sugar would be obtained. Most of the planters in the southern part of the province were convinced that sugar would be the next best article of produce after indigo. Sugar in the southern part of the province was encouraged due to its geographical location. No frost seemed to appear in this region, and the land was rich and fertile.[185]

The public road from St. Augustine to the southern part of the province was still being carried on. Governor Moultrie stated that completion of the road would undoubtedly come about by the winter of 1774. The southern extension of the road now included the northern head of the Indian River.[186]

The province of East Florida, and the settlement at New Smyrna, was going well. Its produce was being exported, and money was being made from Florida products. Under these conditions, Governor Moultrie was informed that Patrick Tonyn, a new governor, had been appointed by His Majesty, George III. On March 19, 1774, Governor Tonyn took his oath of office amidst much pomp and ceremony, and his inauguration was even attended by the Upper Creek Chief, Cowkeeper.[187]

Ten days after taking office Governor Tonyn made an inspection tour of the plantations on the Mosquetto, Tomoka, Hillsborough and Halifax Rivers. He found that the plantations were doing well and the settlement at New Smyrna was growing fine crops of indigo.[188] In the year 1775, however, the indigo crop was far short of that produced the preceding year. This was due to an unusually dry summer that year. A large crop had been grown in the spring of 1774, but it was all ruined by the hot sun. There were, however, many articles of produce exported that year.[189]

A drought ruined the crops at New Smyrna in 1773 also. The drought this year caused Dr. Turnbull to incorporate the use of a new system for crop production. This innovation had never been attempted in the American colonies before. Dr. Turnbull had seen the system used, in the culture of crops in climates similar to that of New Smyrna, with great success. This new system was irrigation, practiced in Egypt and many parts of the ancient world.[190]

The death rate at New Smyrna since 1770 had almost maintained a constant level. In 1771, 10 men and women, and 6 children died; in 1772, 8 men and women, and 3 children died; in 1773, 11 men and women, and 13 children died; and in 1774, 5 men and women, and 19 children died.[191]

Additional income from labor was also coming into the hands of Dr. Turnbull. In 1774 he was also contracted to furnish labor, material and transportation of a sixteen-car boat for the government in St. Augustine. This boat was used to guide ships across the bar in St. Augustine Harbor. Dr. Turnbull received 56.10 pounds for the boat constructed by his colonists.[192]

Although the death rate was decreasing, there was still much dissatisfaction among the colonists, particularly among the Minorcan elements in New Smyrna. The overseer system was still used, and the overseers caused many grievances. Even though crop production was high, there was still hunger among the settlers. Many of them thought of escape to Havana. This idea became known to the English, and the colonists' every move was constantly under surveillance.[193] This was a time of extreme suspicion in all of the English colonies in America, for revolt was feared everywhere.

So great was the Minorcans' misery, that Father Casanovas sided with them in the constant battle of settler versus overseer. He spoke out openly against the commandant and overseers, and for this he was deported to Minorca. Father Camps was left to administer the parish alone, and he was warned not to overstep his bounds by speaking out against the officials of the settlement lest he follow Father Casanovas. The good priest thought of his flock, and dared not desert them in their hour of need. He asked to have another priest sent to New Smyrna to assist him. His attempts were made through numerous letters to his former assistant, Father Casanovas, who failed to answer his letters. A priest from Havana was out of the question, for the English refused to allow one in the province.[194]

Adding to the suspicion and fear that prevailed over the Minorcan colony was the American Revolution that began in 1775. That year saw an alarming increase in the death rate at New Smyrna; 30 men and women, and 21 children died.[195] In this year also, rebel activities caused Governor Tonyn to consider the possibility of using the Minorcans to assist in the defense of the province. In 1776 there were 200 males between the ages of sixteen and fifty. Dr. Turnbull was much concerned with Governor Tonyn's idea of using his settlers. He always considered them to be loyal to His Majesty, and honest enough to fulfill their contracts. He begged that they be allowed to remain on their farms, and that they be protected in their agricultural pursuits. Without their agriculture, the Minorcans and their families would die of starvation.[196]

Relief from their misery was now in sight for the Minorcans. They were no longer concerned with the culture of indigo or sugar cane. Many of them had served their periods of contract and freedom was their only desire. For many, freedom was at hand, freedom from New Smyrna and nothing more. The population of East Florida was increasing daily from the flight of loyalists from the other colonies. This fact would later cause the Minorcans more grief and misery than they had known at New Smyrna, and is a part of another story. Nevertheless, the increase in population in East Florida caused prices to soar and placed an additional burden on the sustenance of the province. More crops were needed and the bare necessities of life were again taken away from the Minorcans. In addition to this, Turnbull left the colony and returned to London to bring complaints against the English authorities in East Florida. He was involved in a heated argument with Governor Tonyn over the latter's conduct in handling a case against his personal friend, Mr. Drayton.

The doctor left his nephew in charge of the settlement during his absence and the brutality of the overseers continued. This young lad could not cope with the settlers and their grievances of hunger and maltreatment.[197] Production continued through 1776 and 1777 with the major portion devoted to indigo. A considerable amount of construction went on at New Smyrna indicating that business was still good. The type of construction gives an idea of the type of production scheduled for New Smyrna's future:

CARPENTER WORK ON SMYRNA SETTLEMENT[198]

22 double sets of Indigo Vats at 50 pounds each	1,100 pounds
One Indigo house	100 pounds
One Wind Mill	300 pounds
One Horse Mill	30 pounds
Two Large Stores for Provisions	500 pounds
4 Bridges, all of cedar at 30 pounds each	120 pounds
Mr. Turnbull's Dwelling House	270 pounds
145 other Houses at 35 pounds each	5,075 pounds
William Watson, Carpenter	Total 7,595 pounds

VI.

New Smyrna, the Indigo Plantation

Indigo is a blue dye obtained from several plants. Natural indigo does not exist in the plants as such, but is obtained by the decomposition of indican, a colorless crystalline glucoside. Indican contains, besides indigotin, various other substances unless it is purified. Indigo is used on fabric fibers, and is the most important vat dye. Indigo itself is obtained from an indigo plant of the genus *indigofera*, also called indigo.

The indigo plant grew wild in East Florida, and its cultivation was undertaken on a very large scale by the English planters. The British government encouraged the manufacturer of Indigo by paying a subsidy to those who produced the blue dye.[199]

The best indigo plant was called flotant or flora. It was light and pure and hardened quickly. It was buoyant, easily inflammable, and its color was a fine dark blue inclined to be violet. By rubbing it with the fingernail, it could be made to assume the color of old copper. The next best indigo plant was called violet, or *gorge de pigeon*. It was heavier in weight than the flora. Both flora and violet were used for dying linen and cotton fabrics. The type of indigo plant most desired by the planters, since it brought the highest price, was of a copper color. This was from the heaviest of all the merchantable indigo plants and therefore its residuum was the best of the three. This copper colored indigo was used especially by the woolen manufacturers.[200]

An indigo plantation was a very unhealthful place to live. The stench at the work vats was so horrible and disagreeable that the location of the "work" was usually one quarter of a mile away from human dwellings. The odor from the rotting weeds drew flies by the thousands. This unhealthy situation probably caused a great deal of illness. It was almost impossible to keep animals and poultry on an indigo plantation, but the manufacturer of indigo was nevertheless a profitable business.[201]

The manufacturing of indigo in eighteenth-century English Florida was a complicated process. It involved a certain amount of skill on the part of the workers. The culture of the plant required care and skill also. The plant required rich, middling, loose soil. The field in which it was to be planted was as level as possible. Indigo will, however, grow in any soil, but rich, moist, hammock or oak land was the best type. The ground had to be thoroughly cleaned and reduced to a perfect garden mould. This was the most laborious part of the plant culture. It was so necessary that no crop could be expected without it.[202]

The best kind of seed was found to be abundant in the Mississippi River region. About four bushels of seed was required for one acre of planting. The seeds were sown in rows and one seed was placed about two feet from the next. The ideal time for sowing was in early March and was continued until early in May, the wet season in East Florida. If the seeds had been sown in early March, and if the season was favorable, five cuttings of the plants could be expected between March and November. No cutting was done during hot, dry weather, for the hot sun destroyed the plants. Rainy, wet weather was the period for cutting. As soon at the plant bloomed it was cut. The blossoms usually appeared about 10 weeks after the seeds were planted. After the plants were cut, they were gathered and tied into bundles and carried to the indigo vats for processing.[203]

The vats were placed one next to the other in sets of three. The first was called the "steeper," and was about sixteen feet square and three feet deep. The second vat was called the "buttery." It was twelve feet square and four and one half feet deep. The third vat was much smaller than the buttery. Three vats of these dimensions could easily handle seven acres of plants in one processing cycle. The vats were constructed of two and one half inch cypress planks, and the joints or studs were of live oak. The planks were well secured by seven-inch spikes. These vats, if constructed as described, could be expected to last at least eight years.[204]

The process of making indigo was relatively simple, though laborious. The plants were tossed into the steeping vat first. They were covered with water from a pump located next to the vat. The plants were pounded in this vat until they began to ferment. The fermentation occurred within eight to twenty hours, depending on the atmosphere. The plants would begin to effervesce violently, and the water in the vat would thicken and assume a purplish-blue color.[205]

One edge of the steeping vat was projected over the beating vat. When the plants began to effervesce in the steeping vat the water was immediately drained into the beating vat. The plants were used no further in the manufacturer, but they could be reprocessed to manufacture saltpetre.[206]

As soon as the liquid entered the beating vat it was stirred by a process similar to churning. This was laborious work and usually performed by Negroes. The beater or churner, as this laborer was called, would draw a lever having one or two bottomless buckets at each end up and down. Horses were used to do this task in some of the larger plantations. The churning was continued until the dying particles separated from the liquid, or until they congealed and formed a mass. It was this part of the process that required care and attention. If the churning ceased before the mass of residue was formed, a part of the dying matter would remain undissolved. If the churning process continued too long, some part of the residue would dissolve again. Only experience in this churning process could teach one when the indigo had been churned enough. The method used to determine when the churning should cease was to pour some of the liquid into a phial or cup and to observe if the dying matter was inclined to dispose of itself or not. To hasten the separation of the residue, some English planters used lime water.[207]

When the indigo had been churned enough the second part of the process was complete, and the residue was allowed to settle to the bottom of the beating vat. The liquid was then drained through a cock fixed at a level higher than the residue into a ditch and used no further. Only the residue and a small amount of liquid remained at the bottom of the beating vat. The residue was then drawn into the third vat through a cock fixed at a level near the bottom of the vat.[208]

The residue was left in the third vat for eight or ten hours, when it was removed from the vat and strained through a horsehair sieve. It was then put into conical shaped bags of cloth called Hippocrates' sleeves, and hung in the shade to drain. These bags contained pure indigo. At this stage the indigo looked like mud. When the water had been drained from the bags their contents were dumped into shallow boxes and placed under the indigo sheds where they were allowed to dry in the shade. When the indigo began to harden it was cut with a thin bladed knife into square pieces. The squares of indigo were left under the drying shed until they were completely dry and hard. This was the state of indigo when it was shipped.[209]

The indigo was carefully turned three or four times a day while it was under the drying shed. Someone had to drive the flies out of the drying shed at all times for too many flies could damage the indigo, particularly when it had not hardened. Extreme care had to be exercised in determining when the indigo was completely dry, and that it was in the shade at all times. If sunlight touched the indigo before it was dry all the tinting matter would be exhaled, and the indigo would be left in a colorless state and assume the color of slate. Care was taken in not allowing the indigo to be near too much moisture. Extreme moisture would keep the indigo dissolved, and cause it to rot.[210]

Although the indigo plant grew wild in East Florida, care and attention had to be given during its period of growth. Two major problems confronted the planter during this period: drought and caterpillars. For drought there was no remedy other then irrigation, and Dr. Turnbull attempted that with reasonable success. The caterpillar was combated by digging a trench three feet wide around the infested part of the field, and the plants within were cut down. The infested portion of the crop was thus isolated. The caterpillars themselves were collected in buckets, drowned in water mixed with lime, and their substance squeezed and strained through a hair sieve. This substance contained indigo also, and it, too, was placed in the drying shed and processed in a manner similar to the indigo derived from the plant itself.[211]

Agricultural production was diversified at New Smyrna. The colony at its inception began to raise crops that would offer the settlers themselves sustenance. As the land was cleared and the colony progressed in age and experience, crop production was placed on a more practical scale. Produce, in addition to that of sustenance, was designed to bring about economic prosperity to both the owners of the settlement and the colonists. New Smyrna, as a business enterprise, gradually limited its production to two crops grown on a large scale. The production of rice was most certainly of major importance in British East Florida, and a high premium was placed on this grain. There is no known record, however, to indicate that this crop was grown at New Smyrna. Sugar was also an important crop in East Florida, though until 1775 it was a matter of mere speculation. Most of the sugar cane was raised near New Orleans. It did, however, yield a high profit, and a considerable amount of sugar cane was raised at New Smyrna.[212] Mention should be made of the commercial production of naval stores, also on a large scale. Almost all of the settlements on the Mosquettos produced naval stores, for the extensive tracts of pine lands in this area offered an almost unlimited supply of tar, pitch, and turpentine. The large wharf and the natural navigation offered by the inland water system to St. Augustine, added more to the feasibility of production of these products. The production of turpentine alone would have been enough to make the economic returns of New Smyrna equal to the rich tobacco-producing colonies farther north.[213] It was the processing of indigo, however, which received the greatest attention at New Smyrna, and to accomplish this thousands of acres of the indigo plant were grown.

Emphasis was placed on the production of indigo almost on the founding of New Smyrna. The province of East Florida, and particularly the area on or near the Mosquetto River, was peculiarly adapted to the culture of the indigo plant. For New Smyrna's production of 1772 alone, a merchant in London paid over 3,000 pounds. The entire annual produce of New Smyrna was usually left to Dr. Turnbull, the manager and co-owner of the colony, to be sold as he saw fit. He either consigned the entire year's production to a merchant in London, or, as was the usual case, he used the annual production as barter for goods supplied by merchants in New York, Philadelphia, and South Carolina. The annual production never failed to receive a return of 3,000 pounds the entire time the colony existed.[214]

It cannot be stated however, that the production of indigo was confined to the settlement of New Smyrna. The chief produce of the entire province of East Florida was indigo, and every plantation of any size devoted most of its land to the cultivation of the indigo plant. The major difficulty encountered by the planters, including Dr. Turnbull, was the actual shipment of indigo. The product itself was so small in bulk and size that the entire production of East Florida was not sufficient to load one vessel. As a result, few vessels appeared in the port of St. Augustine to take a shipment of indigo alone, though the product was of great value, and netted a high return. Bulk seemed to be the main factor considered by ships' captains, and not the value of the cargo. Transportation costs were nigh, and the bulk of the production of East Florida indigo was not usually sufficient to warrant the call of a vessel in the waters of the province. The larger vessels usually went to ports in regions whose produce was much greater and of more bulk than that of East Florida. These ports were much wealthier, and the produce was more diversified. Therefore, if a planter of East Florida had a shipment of indigo, and a vessel did not happen to be in St. Augustine at the time, they were required to pay transportation costs to ship their indigo to another port, usually Charleston. They could, however, leave their indigo at St. Augustine and await the arrival of a vessel that was seeking more freight. If they did this they were forced to pay storage fees. Storage and additional freight costs to another port to effect final shipment to England, plus costs of handling the freight outside the province of East Florida, reduced the planter's profit. Most of the crop of 1773 was shipped to Charleston on the *Pallas*, and the cost of transportation to that port was so high that there was little profit left. No subsidy was given to the planters of indigo in East Florida as was done in some of the other colonies, and this made the loss greater. In 1775 the planters decided to ask for the construction of better port facilities in East Florida, and for a government subsidy for indigo production. The chief spokesman for the group was Colonel James Grant, the former governor of the province of East Florida, who was also a wealthy landowner.[215] Their request was turned down by the Board of Trade the same day that it was made. The Secretary of the Board stated that the request for port facilities and the subsidy were contrary to the "words of the Act of Parliament."[216]

The indigo produce of East Florida for the year 1774 was shipped to London from the port of St. Augustine, on December 24, 1774. Captain Alvara Lefthouse, Master of the brigantine *Betsy*, placed aboard his vessel 12,643 pounds of indigo in 105 casks, 2 chests, 5 boxes, and 4 bags. It is interesting to note that in addition to the indigo and other commodities, several barrels of orange juice was sent to England aboard this vessel. This shipment consisted of 1,633 pounds of indigo from the settlement of New Smyrna.[217]

The export of indigo from East Florida began two years after the New Smyrna settlement was made. The first shipment, made in 1770, was only 6,189 pounds, but the size of the shipments increased annually.[218] New Smyrna furnished its share of indigo shipments. Between the years 1771 and 1777, 43,283 pounds of indigo left the coquina wharfs of the New Smyrna settlement. A breakdown of the export by year shows that a considerable amount of indigo was grown and shipped from New Smyrna. In 1771, 11,558 pounds were exported; 1772, 9,065 pounds; 1773, 10,262 pounds; 1774, 1,633 pounds; 1775, 1,948 pounds; 1776, 6,390 pounds; 1777, 2,397 pounds.[219] It is strange to note that the drought of 1773 did not damage the crop of indigo at New Smyrna, for that was the peak year of that product's export.

Many other products were exported from New Smyrna for use within the province of East Florida and in the colonies to the north. In 1777 the New Smyrna settlement supplied the entire St. Augustine, St. John's River area with over 5,000 bushels of corn.[220] But, Dr. Turnbull's colony was primarily an indigo plantation, and the settlers were learning to manufacture the finished product with great skill, for the indigo they exported made money for the settlement's manager.

VII.

The Minorcans' Exodus

The death rate at New Smyrna increased to alarming proportions in 1776. That year 45 men and women, and 8 children died.[221] The settlers' concern for their lives, their fear of starvation, their resentment of the cruel treatment of the overseers, and their general dissatisfaction were always present at New Smyrna. The settlers in 1776 were still ill clothed and almost destitute of every convenience. Despite the progress made at the colony, most of the people were still living in the same palmetto huts they built on their arrival. The people of New Smyrna began to think again of the homes and the homeland they had left behind eight years before. But, the time was near when some of them could look forward to relief from their contracts. Most of the Italians and Greeks were under the impression that they were to be released at the end of a six-year period.[222] Seven years had passed since they harvested their first crops.

In the background of this inevitable dissatisfaction was the American Revolution that began in 1775 and inflamed the colonies to the north. The English officials had known for some time that the Spaniards desired to regain Florida. Minorcans and Spaniards came within the same scope of culture. On this account, many English officials questioned the loyalty of the Minorcans. They assumed that the Minorcans would desert English Florida and flee to the Spaniards. Suspicion and fear were prevalent during this period. Governor Tonyn feared that the Minorcans would, in their distress, turn to the American rebels for aid. He had been informed that the rebels in Georgia were invited to come to "their relief and deliverance." The Minorcans were purported to have offered their services to the Georgia rebel cause. The plantation owners near the New Smyrna settlement now feared the Minorcans more then ever. Captain Bisset, of *Mount Plenty* plantation on the Mosquetto River, told Governor Tonyn that the Minorcans were not to be trusted with firearms. He advised the Governor to take the most "turbulent" Minorcans into custody in the event the province was invaded by the American patriots.[223]

The death rate in 1777 increased day by day. By the end of the year 72 men and women, and 12 children died.[224] The overseers by this time feared that the English army officers' tempting offers to the dissatisfied settlers would cause them to rise in revolt as they had in 1768. Many offers had been made to the Minorcans to join the Florida Militia against the American patriots.[225] A rumor began in the colony that Dr. Turnbull was trying to cheat his settlers out of the land he had promised them in their contract. They were supposed to receive this land at the end of their agreement. Support of this rumor was to be found in the Proclamation of George III concerning land grants. The land at New Smyrna was supposed to have been settled by Protestant families. The majority at New Smyrna were Roman Catholics, and they assumed that they were not within the terms of Turnbull's contract with the Board of Trade.[226]

Finally, in March, 1777, a large number of New Smyrna inhabitants came to St. Augustine requesting an appointment with Governor Tonyn. They told him of the cruelty that had been imposed upon them, of their extreme hunger, and of their miserable living conditions at New Smyrna. They demanded justice and alleged that their period of service had expired. They stated that the terms of the contract on Dr. Turnbull's part had not been complied with. After hearing their pleas and accusations against Turnbull and his overseers, the governor persuaded them to return to New Smyrna.[227]

This first group of protestors obtained no favorable results from their appointment with the governor.[228] In the latter part of 1777, 90 New Smyrna inhabitants came to St. Augustine, to voice their pleas for aid. Most of them came without their families. Their primary mission was to procure the crop of that year for themselves, for they were hungry. After hearing their case, and presenting arguments in favor of the New Smyrna settlement, the governor finally persuaded them to return. Governor Tonyn told them that it was impossible for all of them to remain. He said that if they thought it would be of benefit to them that they should leave twelve of their number to represent their cause. He prevailed upon them to return, but he had a great deal of difficulty in doing this. He promised them that they would receive a greater allowance of provisions in the future, and that he would see justice received. The settlers reluctantly returned to New Smyrna, leaving behind Anthony Spephonopoli, Nichola Demalache, Giosefa Lurance, Juan Partella, Rafael Hernandes, Michael Alamon, Lewis Capelli, Juan Serra, Rafaiel Simines, Babpina Patchedebourga, Pietro Musquetto, Christopher Flimming, and Lewis Sauche to state their case for them.[229]

As soon as the delegation of 90 settlers arrived in St. Augustine, Governor Tonyn sent for Mr. Gordon, the Attorney General of the province, who was also Dr. Turnbull's attorney. The governor ordered him to settle the entire affair as quickly and efficiently as possible. He also wrote to Mr. Drayton, and told him to hear the settlers' complaints. Drayton failed to answer the governor's directive, but indicated that their complaints ought to be taken before some other magistrate, most probably the Chief Magistrate.[230]

Governor Tonyn at this time felt strongly that success at New Smyrna would never be achieved. He was confident that the loss of all the white settlers would do no damage to the economic success of New Smyrna. Tonyn was convinced that these people's maintenance would always equal the value of their labor as long as the produce went into their own hands. Tonyn had stated on many occasions that if liberated, the settlers at New Smyrna would prove to be industrious settlers within the province.[231]

On May 7 1777, Governor Tonyn directed 18 members of the settlers' delegation to present their testimony before Mr. Henry Younge, a justice of the province. Mr. Younge did not know exactly how to handle their case, for he thought that it was not within his power to assist them. He desired them to make application to some of His Majesty's justices of the peace. Since there was such a great number of deponents, he stated that a complete examination of the case would be long and very troublesome. And so, in order to save the magistrates time and labor, he directed the deponents to commit their complaints in writing to the Clerk of the Pleas, Spencer Man, a justice of the peace for the Province of East Florida. Mr. Younge noted that quite a number of cruelties were going to be recorded, and that several murders had been committed by Turnbull's overseers. So shocked was Mr. Younge that he placed the testimonies of murder before the governor.[232]

Governor Tonyn was now gravely concerned with the past and future conduct of the principals of the New Smyrna settlement. The American patriots in Georgia and their offers to the settlers at New Smyrna could not be forgotten by him. This was a time of trouble. Besides, he and Dr. Turnbull could not get along at all. Dr. Turnbull was in London at that very moment, stating his grievances against Tonyn.

Meanwhile the cases of the settlers from New Smyrna were determined by the courts, which ordered them to be released from their contracts. After the court's decision was rendered, Dr. Turnbull's own attorneys set the entire white population of New Smyrna free. In preparation to receive the new influx of people in St. Augustine, Governor Tonyn directed that small lots of land be available to each family. He was convinced more then ever that in their state of freedom they would become industrious settlers. Much more could be expected from them as free men then was received from them under the "lash of the whip and chains, and in the most abject conditions of oppression and slavery." Thus, by July 26, 1777, the deathblow had been given to the settlement of New Smyrna.[233] Over 40,000 pounds sterling[234] had been expended on the settlement, and ten years after the first settlers arrived in New Smyrna, the cost in human lives was 964.[235]

The actual exodus of the colony from New Smyrna is lost, for there is no recorded description of their movement to St. Augustine. The story is, however, a traditional one among the descendents of the Minorcan colony in St. Augustine. Almost all small children of Minorcan descent have been told it many times. The narrative is as follows:

Sometime in the year 1776 a group of gentlemen from St. Augustine were visiting Dr. Turnbull's plantation. An act of cruelty to one of the laborers was observed by them, and one of them remarked that if these people knew their rights they could obtain freedom. A young lad named Arnau overheard the gentleman's remark and told his mother what he had heard. Mrs. Arnau was quick to spread the word among her friends. It soon reached the ears of the head carpenter, Mr. Pellicer, and he called a meeting of the colony's leading people. The meeting was held at night under the most secret conditions possible. Mr. Pellicer, Mr. Llambias, and Mr. Genoply were selected to represent the people of the colony to the governor in St. Augustine, and to ask that their contracts be terminated due to Turnbull's oppression. In order to cover their absence, the three men worked frantically for days to complete all the tasks they were assigned. When the day of their departure arrived, the three men asked that they be allowed to go to the beach and hunt turtles. The overseer gave them his permission, and the three left New Smyrna early in the morning. Going by way of the beach, and swimming part of the way, they reached Matanzas Inlet the following night. Instead of stopping long enough to rest, the men swam the Inlet and continued their march to St. Augustine, arriving there the next morning.

Upon arriving in St. Augustine the three men went directly to Governor Tonyn, who fed them and offered them dry clothing. They told him of the cruelty and hunger that existed at New Smyrna, and of the deaths that had occurred over the years. The governor, touched by their sad story, bade them to return to New Smyrna and tell their people that the chains of slavery had been broken. This they cheerfully did.

Immediately upon their return, another secret meeting was held in one of the palmetto log huts, and Mr. Pellicer was chosen to lead the Minorcans from New Smyrna. Dr. Turnbull was not present at New Smyrna at this time, but his overseers were, and the Minorcans feared them. One morning, during a northeaster, the whole settlement, taking only the bare minimum of food, began the trek to St. Augustine. Mr. Pellicer formed his group of people in such a way as to protect the older men, the women and the children from the overseers' whips. The group walked a long way from New Smyrna before they were discovered to be missing by the overseers, and on the third day they reached St. Augustine, where provisions were awaiting them. They were thus freed from their contracts with Turnbull.

A certain amount of credence can be given this narrative. There are several histories of old St Augustine. These books were written in the 1850's while the authors resided in St. Augustine. The traditional narrative and the authors' versions closely correspond. This would indicate that they, too, had been told of the "flight" from New Smyrna by a generation of Minorcans born at New Smyrna. At least the narrative was still fresh in their minds and was at most a third-hand story.[236]

Only those who were able to walk left New Smyrna, and many Minorcans remained behind. Though they were freed from their contract by Turnbull's attorneys, they were not physically able to enjoy their new won freedom. Father Camps also remained temporarily at New Smyrna. He felt that he was needed there to care for the ill and hear confessions of those that were about to die, for the disease of dropsy had come to the Minorcans.[237] More hunger was the lot of those who remained in New Smyrna, for their meager rations were cut even shorter. Father Camps suffered more during those days then ever before. He was refused his stipend and the use of his sacred vessels. The ornaments of the church were denied him because he had refused to counsel the settlers to remain in New Smyrna and continue their labors. Eventually the remaining survivors at New Smyrna were taken to St. Augustine by ship. For some unknown reason Father Camps was forced to remain, and not allowed to leave New Smyrna with his parish. In the early part of September, 1777, however, through the intercession of a Spaniard residing in St. Augustine, Father Camps was allowed to leave the Mosquetto settlement and join his parishioners.[238] On November 9, 1777, Father Camps moved his little church of San Pedro to St. Augustine.[239]

Father Camps was the last Minorcan to leave New Smyrna. The *Fromajadas* was never more to be heard on the banks of the irrigation canals of Turnbull's plantation, but will be heard forever in the narrow streets of St. Augustine.

Conclusion

Dr. Turnbull's colony at New Smyrna was a total failure. The underlying cause for its failure centers around an intangible thing commonly called human nature. It was not the American Revolution, nor any other sweeping movements of the times, that brought the deathblow to Turnbull's New Smyrna, but simply the fact that after nine years of misery the people at the settlement wanted to better themselves.

The primary cause of the colonists' dissatisfaction was Turnbull's non-adherence to the contract that he had made with most of them and the maltreatment they suffered Most of them were forced to remain in their contract status, much against their will, after their contract term had expired. This was true, for their cases were tried in courts, and the magistrate's decision was that their contract was to be terminated. The majority of the people fell into this category according to the testimony given by the eighteen-member delegation from New Smyrna. Once the courts rendered their decision the die was cast, and Turnbull severed his contract with the others.

The settlers had many grievances, all of which revolved around inhuman treatment by both Turnbull and his overseers. This maltreatment of the settlers cannot be overlooked, for it was a major cause of their break with Andrew Turnbull, though not the primary one. The murders that were committed likewise cannot be overlooked, for they were duly considered by the courts in rendering their decision. As a result, the settlers were released from their contracts, and New Smyrna was largely depopulated.

The members of the New Smyrna colony were not slaves, servants, nor criminals, but free people who had signed contracts with Dr. Turnbull to work his land as "farmers" for a specific number of years. After the term of their contract was fulfilled, these people themselves became landowners, and during the term of their contract they were entitled to a percentage of the produce of the land they worked. There is a great deal of misconception in the point that these people were servants, slaves, and many other things, which they actually were not. It should be pointed out that a contract colony was nothing new to British North America. Many of the colonies founded long before New Smyrna were based on the same principle. The colony at Jamestown is one of the better examples. No one from that settlement has ever been called a servant or slave because he signed a contract to settle that area. On the contrary, he might probably be considered today a founder of one of the First Families of America.

New Smyrna was actually a sound economic enterprise, and under proper management, it might have survived without its white settlers. There was, as indicated by the returns from shipments of indigo and other products, a considerable amount of money made from the produce of the colony. It is remarkable that a colony of such a large number of people could have survived as long as it actually did, considering the poor logistical planning for its arrival at East Florida. There was little land prepared for them to plant, and it required time to clear the land and raise crops.

It is even more remarkable that the colony progressed as well as it did despite the language difficulty with which the colonists were confronted, for Greek, Catalan and Italian are different languages. They solved the problem somehow for they encountered the problem in Mahon in 1767, and in New Smyrna they lived with it for ten years.

In religion, quite a few Greeks were converted to Roman Catholicism as indicated in Fathers Camps's register. Many Greek names appear as godparents, a fact that indicates that many were converted to Roman Catholicism. Conversion of these people came about through inter-marriage and through the popularity and good works of Father Camps and Father Cassonovas, and from the use of the little Church of San Pedro as a meeting place for all social activities of the colony.

The numerous deaths at the colony were caused by scurvy, hunger, and dropsy as indicated in the manuscripts. Many were undoubtedly caused by the unsanitary conditions. It was primarily an indigo plantation, and the unsanitary conditions of the sheds and works have already been pointed out. Rotting

Conclusion

matter caused flies, rodents and numerous other insects to infest the site of the work. Modern medicine has proven that many diseases are carried by flies, mosquitoes, fleas, ticks and rats. There were probably many deaths caused by yellow fever, typhoid fever, and malaria. Many people at the colony were weakened by the meager diet they were given to sustain themselves, and they therefore were especially susceptible to disease. It is a small wonder that they were not plagued with an epidemic. It should also be noted that many deaths were probably caused by pneumonia. The settlers were required to work in wet weather sowing seeds and cutting the indigo plants. The weather during sowing time was cold. There was a lack of meat in their diet, for no animals or poultry could be raised on an indigo plantation. The people of New Smyrna were always ill clothed. Most of them were half naked through 1776.

Andrew Turnbull did not live up to the contract he made with his settlers. He promised them sustenance, a livelihood, his attention to their care, and all the necessities of life. He did not give them these, and this fact caused more dissatisfaction than the manuscripts mention. He also stated that the settlers were to be farmers, and made no mention of the duties that would be imposed on them as indigo laborers. Some of them undoubtedly became quite skilled at the beating vat, but in the main they were subjected to work normally assigned to Negro slaves. The dissatisfaction turned to hate for Turnbull and his overseers.

The English government was much interested in the successful outcome of the settlement of New Smyrna. Every encouragement was given to Turnbull, for he received considerable aid from both the provincial government and the crown. In 1770, the government in London finally became convinced that the colony would collapse, and no more financial aid was given by His Majesty. The government's reasons for this decision require further study. Turnbull was on his own as far as the government was concerned when Tonyn arrived and became governor of East Florida.

Not all of the settlers left New Smyrna in 1777, and the settlement itself was not completely closed down as far as operations were concerned. It is known that produce continued to be exported from the settlement, and therefore, it must be concluded that the indigo works were still in operation. There were people there, and New Smyrna exists today. The colonists who left New Smyrna and came to St. Augustine were not all the settlers at New Smyrna. But this is another story and can be mentioned but briefly here. The story of the Minorcans in St. Augustine also belongs to another study. Most of them remained in St. Augustine, and their descendents form a considerable part of the population of that city today.

Notes

Introduction
1. T.S. Ashton, *The Industrial Revolution, 1760–1830* (London: Oxford University Press, 1958), pp. 4–22.
2. Charles Moran, *The Sea of Memories: The Story of Mediterranean Strife Past and Present,* (New York: Scribner's Sons, 1942), pp. 83–84.

Chapter I
3. Arthur L. Cross, *A Shorter History of England and Greater Britain* (New York: Macmillan Co., 1942), pp. 509–510. See also Carlton J.H. Hayes, Marchall W. Baldwin, and Charles W. Cole, *History of Europe* (rev. ed., New York: Macmillan Co., 1956), pp. 645–646. An analysis of Spain's rivalry with England is given in Homer C. Hackett and Arthur M. Schlesinger, *Land of the Free, A Short History of the American People* (New York; Macmillan Co., 1947), pp. 33–34.
4. This was defined in the Proclamation of George III and was named the Proclamation of October 7, 1763.
5. Charles L. Mowat, *East Florida as a British Province, 1763–1784* (Berkeley: University of California Press, 1943), pp. 3–4.
6. *Georgia Gazette*, April 14, 1763, a dispatch from Charleston, March 30, 1763.
7. Captain Hodges's name is yet not clear. Existing records indicate two spellings, offering two pronunciations. The other spelling s Hedges.
8. MSS, (Class) 34 vol. 55, Public Record Office, Index to the Amherst Papers which constitute War Office, Letter of Reppel to Amherst, July 3, 1763. A typewritten copy in St. Augustine Historical Society Library, St. Augustine, Florida.
9. MSS, Colonial Office Papers Class 5, vol. 548, p 13. Letter of Major Ogilvie to the Secretary of State, St. Augustine, August 1, 1763. References made to manuscripts in Colonial Office Papers will hereafter be cited as C.O. with class and volume number cited as 5/548.
10. MSS, Archive General de Indias, Santo Domingo, estante 86, cajon 7, legajo 11, Letter of Melchior Feliu to Count de Richla, St. Augustine, August 25, 1763. A translated copy now exists in the St. Augustine Historical Society Library, St. Augustine, Florida.

11. Mowat, co. cit., pp. 7–10.

12. C.O. 5/540, p. 135, Ogilvie to Board of Trade, St. Augustine, January 26, 1764.

13. Mowat, op. cit., pp. 10–11.

14. Adam Shortt and Arthur G. Doughty, *Constitutional History of Canada* (Ottawa, 1918), vol. I, p. 150.

15. Ibid.

16. Mowat, op. cit., p. 54.

17. *Georgia Gazette*, December 27, 1764.

18. Mowat, op. cit., p. 55.

19. Shortt and Doughty, op. cit., p. 151.

20. *Georgia Gazette*, December 27, 1764, op. cit.

21. E.W. Lawson, 'Minorcans of St. Augustine" (unpublished paper read to St. Augustine Historical Society, December 14, 1948).

22. *Georgia Gazette*, December 27, 1764, op. cit.

23. Ibid.

24. Charles L. Mowat, "That Odd Being, De Brahm," *Florida Historical Quarterly*, xx (April, 1942), pp 323–345. For the unpublished part of De Brahm's "Report," see Carita D. Corse, "De Brahm's Report on East Florida, 1773," *Florida Historical Quarterly*, XVII (January, 1939), pp. 219–226.

25. Mowat, op. cit., p. 58.

26. C.O. 5/548, p. 297, undated, Petition of William Stork to Crown. C.O. 5/540, pp 147–151, 155, 157, Mr. Cressener's Letter on plans of M. Vivegnis to Board of Trade, June 24, 1764, transmitted to Board July 13, 1764.

27. C.O. 5/540, pp 425–426, an enclosure in Governor Grant's report to Board of Trade, St. Augustine, November 22, 1764. This proposal of John Savage is a very controversial subject. Some sources insist that the colony did in fact exist in 1766. More investigation is needed on this subject.

28. C.O. 5/540, pp. 425–426, Petition of Ephraim and John Gilbert enclosed in Governor Grant to Board of Trade, St. Augustine, July 16, 1765.

29. Mowat, op. cit., p. 63.

30. C.O. 5/557, pp. 51–53, an enclosure in letter of Governor Tonyn to Lord Germain, St. Augustine, November, 1776.

Chapter II

31. Carita (Doggett) Corse, *Dr. Andrew Turnbull and the New Smyrna Colony* (Jacksonville: Drew Press, 1919), p. 16.

32. Edward W. Lawson, "Minorcans of St. Augustine" (unpublished paper read to St. Augustine Historical Society, December 14, 1948).

33. Corse, loc. cit.

34. William H. Siebert, *Loyalist in East Florida, 1774 to 1778* (Deland, 1929), II, 56, no. 50.

35. E.P. Panagopoulos, "The Background of the Greek Settlers in the New Smyrna Colony," *Florida Historical Quarterly*, XXV, no. 2, (October 1956), pp. 95–98. Also, "Narrative of Dr. Turnbull," in Lanadowne MSS, LXXXVIII, p. 133. A typed copy of the MSS in St. Augustine Historical Society Library, St. Augustine, Florida.

36. Corse, loc. cit.

37. Panagopolous, op. cit., p. 97. Lord Shelburne, however was not Secretary of State but President of the Board of Trade, see Mowat, op. cit., p. 16.

38. Panagopolous, op. cit., p.98, and Corse, op. cit., p. 18. Also MSS, Treasury 77/7, Memorial and East Florida Claims of Grenville and Lucy Mary Duncan, London, December 30, 1786.

39. MSS 77/7, London, December 30, 1786, op. cit.

40. C.O. 5/548, No. 23, undated.

41. C.O. 5/548, No. 285, Governor Grant to Earl of Shelburne, St. Augustine, January 20, 1767.

42. Ibid. The "Mosquettos' can be defined as two separate branches of the inland waterway on the East Coast of Florida. The north part of Mosquetto begins at Mantanzas Inlet and the south part a little north of Cape Canaveral. The origin of the name of Mosquettos is unknown. The Indians called it Muscoso, the Spaniards named it Mosquito and the English accepted the Anglicized term of Mosquetto. On the east bank of the Mosquetto is a narrow strip of land separating the ocean from the river as far south as Playinda Beach, Florida. There are many small islands in the middle of the river. The Mosquitto Lagoon still exists. The western bank of this lagoon may be viewed completely by automobile from Highway U.S. A-1A. The intra-coastal waterway portion of Mosquitto Lagoon ends at a place called Allenhurst, Florida.

43. Bernard Romans, *Natural History of East and West Florida* (New York, 1775), p. 268. A typed script copy of parts of this work in 2 vols., located in P.E. Younge Library of Florida History, University of Florida, Gainesville, Florida.

44. Ibid.

45. Ibid.

46. King's MSS. 211, p 229, undated. This manuscript is in the British Museum, London. A typed copy of parts of this manuscript are in the St. Augustine Historical Society Library, St. Augustine, Florida. The page cited also shows a map plan of "Mukoso Inlet and Environs" as surveyed in 1765 and 1767.

47. William G. DeBrahm, *History of the Three Provinces, South Carolina, Georgia and East Florida*, p. 294. The manuscript is in Harvard College Library. A typed copy of this work in St. Augustine Historical Library, St. Augustine, Florida.

48. C.O. 5/541 Governor Grant to Lords of Trade, St. Augustine, April 26, 1766. See also William Bartram, *Travels of William Bartram*, Mark Van Doren, ed. New York: Dover Publications, 1959, p. 134.

49. Bartram, loc. cit.

50. Governor Grant to Earl of Shelburne, St. Augustine, January 20, 1767, op. cit.

51. Ibid.

52. Corse, op. cit., p. 20.

53. Governor Grant to Earl of Shelburne, St. Augustine, January 20, 1767, op. cit.

54. Lansdowne Mss LII, p. 294, Governor James Grant to the Earl of Shelburne, St. Augustine, January 17, 1767.

55. Governor Grant to Earl of Shelburne, St. Augustine, January 1767, op. cit.

56. Panagopolous, op. cit., p. 99.

57. C.O. 5/541, p. 272, undated. An extract from "Return of grants of land passed in His Majesty's Province of East Florida, from June 20, 1765 to June 22, 1767." Another grant of 2,000 acres is awarded to Turnbull on the same document cites the Family Rite Order signed June 15, 1776. It states that there were 4 Blacks in the family, and the quit rent is due on the Feast of St. Michael, 1769.

58. C.O. 5/548, Enclosure "I, undated and enclosed in letter of Governor Grant to Earl of Shelburne, St. Augustine, January 20, 1767, op. cit. This enclosed letter is signed by Andrew Turnbull, addressed to the Board of Trade. It was endorsed by the Board March 31, 1767. It is apparent that this petition was written by Turnbull while he was still in St. Augustine by virtue of it being enclosed in the correspondence of Governor Grant. Its context reads as though Turnbull had recently arrived in England. See also Corse, op. cit., p. 27.

59. MSS, Treasury 77/7, March 9, 1781. Lord George Grenville was not Prime Minister of England at this time, Lord Crafton was. Lord Grenville had been Prime Minister (1763–1765), but proved to be very unpopular with both parliament and King George III. The Stamp Act involving the American Colonies was passed during his ministry. See Cross, op. cit., pp 517–518.

60. MSS Treasury 77/7, March 9, 1781, op. cit., MSS Treasury 77/7 Memorial and East Florida Claims of Grenville and Lady Mary Duncan, London, December 30, 1786, *op. cit.*; Corse, op. cit., pp 17, 27.

61. MSS Treasury 77/7, December 30, 1786, op. cit.

62. Governor Grant to Lord Shelburne, St. Augustine, January 20, 1767, op. cit.

63. Enclosure No. 1 in Governor Grant to Earl of Shelburne, St. Augustine, March 31, 1767, op. cit.

64. C.O. 5/548, p. 305, Lords of Trade to the Earl of Shelburne, Whitehall, April 7, 1767.

65. C.O. 5/548 p. 309, Turnbull to the Crown, Memorial of Andrew Turnbull, London, endorsed by Lords of Trade April 9, 1767.

66. C.O. 5/548, p. 313, Lords of Trade to the Earl of Shelburne, April 16, 1767.

67. C.O. 5/548, p. 229, Lords of Trade to the Earl of Shelburne, April 16, 1767.

68. C.O. 5/548, Letter No. 8, Earl of Shelburne to Governor Grant, Whitehall, May 14, 1767.

69. MSS, Privy Council Register, vol. 112, the entry of May 13, 1767. A typed copy of this entry is in the St. Augustine Historical Society Library, St. Augustine, Florida.

70. MSS, American State Papers, vol. 3, pp. 800-801. List of grants by the British Government to Andrew Turnbull at New Smyrna, 1767–1775, for which resumption of title was applied for by his heirs to the Commissioner of Land Claims of the United States, December 20, 1827. A typed extract copy of pp. 800–801 of the above cited is in the St. Augustine Historical Society Library, St. Augustine, Florida.

71. Panagopolous, op. cit., p. 101.

Chapter III

72. Lansdowne MSS, LXXXVIII, folio 141, Andrew Turnbull to Earl of Shelburne, Leghorn, June 15, 1767.

73. Ibid.

74. Johann David Schopf, *Reise durch Einge der Mittlern und Sudlichen Vereinigten Nordamerikanishchen Staaten Mach Ost –Florida un de Bahama Inselin* (Erlanger, 1788). An English translation of this work was used, *Travels in the Confederation. 1783–1784*, trans. and ed. A.J. Morrison (Philadelphia, 1911), pp. 233–237. No copy of a written contract between Turnbull and the Italians at Leghorn had been found. Some of the original Italian colonists stated that they had actually signed a contract. Others stated that there was no contract, only a verbal agreement.

75. Lansdowne MSS, LXXXVIII, folio 135, Andrew Turnbull to Earl of Shelburne, Port Mahon, July 10, 1767.

76. Ibid.

77. Lansdowne MSS, LXXXVIII, folio 147, Andrew Turnbull to Earl of Shelburne, Minorca, February 27, 1768.

78. Ibid.

79. Ibid.

80. C.O. 5/549, p. 77, Governor Grant to Earl of Shelburne, St. Augustine, March 12, 1768.

81. Andrew Turnbull to Earl of Shelburne, Minorca, February 27, 1768, op. cit.

82. Panagopolous, op. cit., pp. 101–107.

83. Andrew Turnbull to Earl of Shelburne, Minorca, February 27, 1768, op. cit.

84. Ibid.

85. Ibid.

86. Panagopolous, op. cit., pp. 111–113.

87. Ibid.

88. MSS, Turnbull Contract Made In Minorca, Mahon, February 11, 1768. A typed copy in St. Augustine Historical Society Library, St. Augustine, Florida.

89. Andrew Turnbull to Earl of Shelburne, Minorca, February 27, 1768, op. cit.

90. Reverend Michael J. Curley, Church and State in the Spanish Floridas, 1783–1822 (Washington: Catholic University Press, 1940), p. 25.

91. Lords of Trade to Earl of Shelburne, Whitehall, April 16, 1767, op. cit.

92. Curley, op. cit, p. 26.

93. Ibid.

94. Andrew Turnbull to Earl of Shelburne, Minorca, February 27, 1768, op. cit.

95. De Brahm, op. cit., pp. 315–316.

96. Andrew Turnbull to Earl of Shelburne, Minorca, February 27, 1768, op. cit.

97. Lansdowne MSS, LXXXVIII, folio 151, Andrew Turnbull to Earl of Shelburne, Minorca, March 28, 1768.

98. Ibid.

99. Lansdowne MSS, LXXXVIII, folio 145, Andrew Turnbull to Earl of Shelburne, Gibraltar, April 4, 1768.

100. Ibid.

101. C.O. 5/549, p. 257, an enclosure in a letter of Governor Grant to Lord Hillsborough, St. Augustine, July 2, 1768.

102. Andrew Turnbull to Earl of Shelburne, Gibraltar, April 4, 1768, op. cit.

103. C.O. 5/549, p. 253, Governor Grant to Lord Hillsborough, St. Augustine, July 2, 1768.

Chapter IV

104. C.O. 5/549, p. 77, Governor Grant to Earl of Shelburne, St. Augustine, March 12, 1768.

105. C.O. 5/549, not numbered. Lord Hillsborough to Governor Grant, St. London, May 12, 1768.

106. C.O. 5/549, p. 253, Governor Grant to Lord Hillsborough, St. Augustine, July 2, 1768. op. cit.

107. Ibid.

108. C.O. 5/549, p. 107, an enclosure in Governor Tonyn to Lord Hillsborough, St. Augustine, July 15, 1778.

109. Corse, op. cit.

110. Morrison, *Travels in the Confederation*, op. cit., pp 233–236.

111. Ibid.

112. C.O., 5/549, No. 9, Governor Grant to Lord Hillsborough, St. Augustine, August 29, 1768.

113. Ibid.

114. Governor Grant to Lord Hillsborough, St. Augustine, July 2, 1768, op. cit.

115. Ibid.

116. Ibid.

117. Curley, op. cit., p. 29; Governor Grant to Lord Hillsborough, St. Augustine, August 29, 1768, op. cit

118. Romans, op. cit.

119. Governor Grant to Lord Hillsborough, St. Augustine, July 2, 1768, op. cit.

120. Ibid.

121. C.O., 5/550, No. 15, Governor Grant to Lord Hillsborough, St. Augustine, December 1, 1768.

122. Corse, op. cit., p. 45.

123. Governor Grant to Lord Hillsborough, St. Augustine, July 2, 1768, op. cit.

124. C.O., 5/549, No. 9, Governor Grant to Lord Hillsborough, St. Augustine, August 29, 1768. This manuscript gives the description of the uprising of the colony in great detail.

125. Romans, op. cit., p. 271.

126. Governor Grant to Lord Hillsborough, St. Augustine, August 29, 1768, op. cit.

127. Ibid.

128. Ibid.

129. C.O., 5/550, No. 14, Governor Grant to Lord Hillsborough, St. Augustine, October 20, 1768.

130. C.O., 5/550, No. 24, Governor Grant to Lord Hillsborough, St. Augustine, January 14, 1768.

131. C.O., 5/550, No. 30, Governor Grant to Lord Hillsborough, St. Augustine, July 20, 1769.

132. Ibid.

133. Romans, op. cit., p. 272.

134. C.O., 5/550, No. 26, Lord Hillsborough to Governor Grant, London, November 2, 1769.

135. Governor Grant to Lord Hillsborough, St. Augustine, August 29, 1768, op. cit.

136. Romans, op. cit. p.272.

137. Governor Grant to Lord Hillsborough, St. Augustine, August 29, 1768, op. cit.

Chapter V

138. Governor Tonyn to Lord Germain, St. Augustine, January 15, 1778, op. cit

139. Governor Grant to Lord Hillsborough, St. Augustine, December 1, 1768, op. cit.

140. Ibid.

141. Ibid.

142. DeBrahm, op. cit., p. 315.

143. Curley op. cit., pp 35-36.

144. Ibid.

145. C.O., 5/551, No. 39, Governor Grant to Lord Hillsborough, St. Augustine, September 1, 1770.

.146. Governor Grant to Lord Hillsborough, St. Augustine, December 1, 1768, op. cit.

147. Ibid.

148. Romans, op. cit., p. 269.

149. Governor Grant to Lord Hillsborough, St. Augustine, December 1, 1768, op. cit.

150. Lansdowne MSS, LXXXVIII, folio 155, Andrew Turnbull to Earl of Shelburne, New Smyrna, September 24, 1769.

151. C.O., 5/550, No. 26, Governor Grant to Lord Hillsborough, St. Augustine, March 4, 1769.

152. C.O., 5/550, not designated, an affidavit of Thomas Bradshaw, Treasurer, March 30, 1769.

153. C.O., 5/550, No. 24, Lord Hillsborough to Governor Grant, London, April 3, 1769.

154. C.O., 5/550, undesignated, Lord Hillsborough to Governor Grant, London, June 7, 1769

155. C.O., 5/550, No. 30, Governor Grant to Lord Hillsborough, St. Augustine, July 20, 1769.

156. Governor Grant to Lord Hillsborough, St. Augustine, September 1, 1770, op. cit.

157. Governor Tonyn to Lord Germain, St. Augustine, January 15, 1778, op. cit

158. Governor Grant to Lord Hillsborough, St. Augustine, September 1, 1769, op. cit.

159. Ibid.

160. Ibid.

161. Ibid.

162. C.O. 5/552, No. 45, duplicate of accounts and vouchers, an enclosure in Governor Grant to Lord Hillsborough, St. Augustine, February 15, 1771.

163. C.O., 5/551, no. 35, Lord Hillsborough to Governor Grant, London, December 11, 1770.

164. C.O., 5/551, and enclosure, Grey Cooper to the Lords of Trade, London, December 13, 1770.

165. C.O., 5/552, undesignated, John Robinson to Mr. Powell, London, March 8, 1771.

166. C.O., 5/552, No. 46, Governor Grant to Lord Hillsborough, St. Augustine, March 20, 1771.

167. Governor Tonyn to Lord Germain, St. Augustine, January 15, 1778, op. cit.

168. Howat, op. cit., p. 16.

169. C.O., 5/552, No. 44, Governor Grant to Lord Hillsborough, St. Augustine, December 14, 1770.

170. C.O., 5/552, No. 3, Lt. Governor Moultrie to Lord Hillsborough, St. Augustine, June 13, 1771.

171. C.O., 5/552, p. 97, Andrew Turnbull to Lt. Governor Moultrie, New Smyrna, May 9, 1771.

172. Ibid.
173. Ibid.
174. C.O. 5/552, p. 101, a copy of a letter from Lt. Governor Moultrie to Major MacKenzie, St. Augustine, June 6, 1771.
175. Ibid.
176. C.O. 5/552, No. 43, Lord Hillsborough to Lt. Governor Moultrie, London, December 4, 1771.
177. C.O. 5/552, No. 6, Lt. Governor Moultrie to Lord Hillsborough, St. Augustine, September 25, 1771.
178. Ibid.
179. C.O. 5/552, No. 44, Lord Hillsborough to Lt. Governor Moultrie, London, January 11, 1772.
180. C.O. 5/552, No. 10, Lt. Governor Moultrie to Lord Hillsborough, St. Augustine, December 28, 1771.
181. C.O. 5/552, No. 18, Lt Governor Moultrie to Earl of Dartmouth, St. Augustine, Augustine, August 28, 1772.
182. Curley, op. cit., p. 34.
183. Corse, op. cit., p. 76.
184. Governor Grant to Lord Hillsborough, St. Augustine, December 14, 1770, op. cit.
185. C.O. 5/553, No. 23, Lt. Governor Moultrie to Earl of Dartmouth, St. Augustine, February 18, 1773.
186. Ibid.
187. C.O. 5/554, No. 2, Governor Tonyn to Earl of Dartmouth, St. Augustine, March 27, 1774.
188. C.O. 5/554, No. 3, Governor Tonyn to Earl of Dartmouth, St. Augustine, March 29, 1774.
189. C.O. 5/555, No. 13, Governor Tonyn to Earl of Dartmouth, St. Augustine, January 23, 1775.
190. Lansdowne MSS, LXXXVIII, folio 157, Andrew Turnbull to Earl of Shelburne, New Smyrna, October 3, 1774.
191. Governor Tonyn to Lord Germain, St. Augustine, January 15, 1778, op. cit
192. C.O. 5/555, No. 205, Governor Tonyn to Lord Germain, St. Augustine, July 19, 1775.
193. C.O. 5/557, a copy of the testimony of Eichola Demalache, Giosefa Marcatto, Rafel Hernandes, and Pompey Possi, May 7, 1777. These testimonies appear as enclosures in Governor Tonyn to Lord Germain, St Augustine, May 8, 1777.
194. Curley, op. cit., p. 35.
195. Governor Tonyn to Lord Germain, St. Augustine, January 15, 1778, op. cit.
196. C.O., 5/556, p. 105, Andrew Turnbull Governor Tonyn, New Smyrna, March 7, 1776.
197. Corse, op. cit., p. 142.
198. MSS Treasury 77/7, 1777, undesignated, a list of work done on Smyrna settlement during 1777. A typed copy of this in Mrs. Corse's notes, presented to the St. Augustine Historical Society, and entitled the Shelburne Papers.

Chapter VI
199. Wilbur H. Siebert, "Slavery and White Servitude in East Florida, 1726–1776," *Florida Historical Quarterly*, X, No. 1 (July 1931), p. 21.
200. Romans, op. cit., pp. 134–139.
201. Ibid.
202. Ibid.
203. Ibid.
204. Ibid.
205. Ibid.

206. Ibid.
207. Ibid.
208. Ibid.
209. Ibid.
210. Ibid.
211. De Brahm, op. cit., p. 310, the footnote.
212. MSS, Treasury 77/7, Memorial and East Florida Claims of Lord Grenville and Lady Mary Duncan, London, December 30, 1786, op. cit.
213. Ibid.
214. Ibid.
215. C.O. 5/555, pp. 127–132, Colonel James Grant to Earl of Dartmouth, London May 24, 1775. This is a memorial of James Grant and other planters in East Florida.
216. C.O. 5/555, pp. 135, endorsement by Secretary of the Board of Trade on Memorial of Colonel James Grant and other planters in East Florida, London, May 24, 1775.
217. C.O. 5/555, pp. 101, enclosure in Governor Tonyn to Earl of Dartmouth, St. Augustine, January 23, 1775.
218. C.O. 5/555, pp. 101–103, enclosure in Governor Tonyn to Earl of Dartmouth, St. Augustine, January 23, 1775.
219. C.O. 5/558,No. 49, p. 111, enclosure # 1 in Governor Tonyn to Earl of Dartmouth, St. Augustine, January 24, 1778.
220. MSS, Sackville HHS, American, 1755–1777, No. 100, Turnbull to Lord George Germain, St. Augustine, December 5, 1777.

Chapter VII
221. Governor Tonyn to Lord Germain, St. Augustine, January 15, 1778, op. cit.
222. C.O. 5/557, No. 39, enclosure #2, testimony of Anthony Stephonopoli in letter of Governor Tonyn to Lord Germain, St. Augustine, May 8, 1777.
223. C.O. 5/557, No. 39, Governor Tonyn to Lord Germain, St. Augustine, May 8, 1777.
224. Governor Tonyn to Lord Germain, St. Augustine, January 15, 1778, op. cit.
225. Siebert, op. cit., Vol. 1, p.38.
226. Corse, op. cit., p. 147.
227. Governor Tonyn to Lord Germain, St. Augustine, May 8, 1777, op. cit.
228. Ibid.
229. Ibid., also enclosures #1–21.
230. Governor Tonyn to Lord Germain, St. Augustine, May 8, 1777, op. cit.
231. Ibid.
232. C.O. 5/557, p. 625, letter of Justice Henry Younge to Governor Tonyn, St. Augustine, May 8, 1777.
233. C.O. 5/557, p. 42, Governor Tonyn to Lord Germain, St. Augustine, July 26, 1777.
234. C.O. 5/558, p. 49, Governor Tonyn to Lord Germain, St. Augustine, December 29, 1777.
235. Governor Tonyn to Lord Germain, St. Augustine, January 15, 1778, op. cit.
236. This narrative is traditional, and I have written it from memory, for I have heard this story many times, and have always been intrigued by it. See Charles Reynolds, Old St. Augustine, a Story of Three Centuries (St. Augustine, 1885), pp. 88–90; also William W. Dewhurst, *The History of St. Augustine,* Florida (New York: G. P. Putnam's Sons, 1885), pp. 118–119.
237. Governor Tonyn to Lord Germain, St. Augustine, December 29, 1777, op. cit.
238. Curley, op. cit., pp. 39–40.
239. Father Camps's Register of Births 1768–1783, New Smyrna and St. Augustine, Entry of November 1777.

Bibliography

Manuscripts

The principal source of information for this study of the Minorcan colony was found in microfilm copies of transcripts of English governmental documents. These documents are to be found in the Public Record Office in London. Photostats of these official papers, as pertains to British East Florida, are to be found in the Library of Congress in Washington. The principal series are classified as Colonial Office Papers, Class 5, Volumes 540 to 573 (cited as C.O. 5/540, etc. in the endnotes of the text), and are devoted to East Florida. The photostatic copies of the Colonial Office Papers were microfilmed by the Saint Augustine Historical Society, and the reels are located in their library in St. Augustine, Florida.

Additional Manuscripts

Endnotes in the text cite manuscripts from the Treasury Papers, Lansdowne MSS, King's MSS, American State Papers, Privy Council Register, and Sackville MSS. The Treasury Papers are deposited in the Public Records Office, London, and only a few photostats of these documents are deposited in the Library of Congress, The Lansdowne MSS is contained in the Shelburne Papers, and is deposited in the William L. Clements Library of the University of Michigan, at Ann Arbor. The Privy Council Register is located in the Public Records Office, London and photostats of parts of the Register are found in the Library of Congress. Photostats of the Sackville MSS are also deposited in the Library of Congress. The American State Papers are in the National Archives,

Washington, D.C., and contain documents relating to the transfer of Florida to the United States in 1821, in which property granted under the British was involved.

The King's Manuscript is deposited in the British Museum, London. De Brahms's <u>Report of the General Survey in the Southern District of North America </u>is King's MSS, Nos. 210, 211, of which several citations are made in this study. The Harvard University Library has a manuscript of De Brahm's *Report*, in a bound volume entitled *Brahm's Survey of East Florida, Carolina, Georgia*, etc.; also a manuscript volume of De Brahm's <u>Continuation of the Atlantic Pilot</u>.

All references made to the aforementioned manuscripts are from typed copies, or extracts of the manuscripts themselves. These copies and extracts are possessed by the St. Augustine Historical Society, and are deposited in their library. They may be found in a file folder entitled "Shelburne Papers." These copies were presented to the society by Mrs. Carita Doggett Corse, and was material collected by her in preparing her *Dr. Andrew Turnbull and the New Smyrna Colony.*

Andrew Turnbull's "Contract With the Minorcans," Mahon, February 11, 1768, is deposited in an archive in Mahon, Minorca. A copy of this contract is in the St. Augustine Historical Society Library, St. Augustine.

The manuscript cited Archivo General de Indias, Santo Domingo, estante 86, camon 7, legajo 11, no. 11 (AGI:SD 86-7-11) is deposited in the Archive of the Indes, Seville, Spain. A typed copy is in the library of the Saint Augustine Historical Society, and has been translated by Mr. E.W. Lawson. The Spanish typed copy was used in this study, and not the translation.

Register of Father Camps, 1768–1783
This register contains a list, by date, of all baptisms performed by both Fathers Camps and Casanovas for the years 1768–1783. It gives a wealth of information pertaining to the Roman Catholic elements of the New Smyrna Colony. This register was located in the Cathedral Rectory, St. Augustine, Florida for a number of years, and is presently located in the Library of the University of Notre Dame at South Bend, Indiana. The Register is also known by the more familiar title of "The Golden Book of the Minorcans," a title given it by a priest, Monsignor James Nunan. The register has been microfilmed, and a reel of the film may be obtained from the St. Augustine Historical Society; Library of Florida History, Gainesville; the Castillo de San Marcos, St. Augustine, and the University Library, University of Notre Dame, South Bend, Indiana.

Newspapers
Georgia Gazette. Savannah Georgia. Articles in editions of April 14, 1763 and December 27, 1764. (A complete series of publications during the period of British possession of Florida exists in microfilm and may be obtained at the Library of the Georgia Historical Society Savannah, Georgia.)

Books

Ashton, T.S. *The Industrial Revolution, 1760–1830*. London: Oxford University Press.

Corse, Carita Doggett. *Dr. Andrew Turnbull and the New Smyrna Colony*. Jacksonville: Drew Press, 1919.

Cross, Arthur L. *A Shorter History of England and Greater Britain*. New York: Macmillan Company, 1942.

Curley, Rev. Michael J. *Church and State in the Spanish Floridas, 1783–1822*. A published doctoral dissertation. Washington: Catholic University Press, 1940.

De Brahm, William G. *History of the Three Provinces, South Carolina, Georgia, and East Florida*. A typed copy of this work is in the St. Augustine Historical Society Library.

Dewhurst, William W. *The History of St. Augustine, Florida*. New York: G.P. Putnam's Sons, 1885.

Hayes, Carlton J. H., et. al. *History of Europe*. Revised edition. New York: Macmillan Company, 1956.

Bockett, Homer C., and Arthur H. Schlessinger. *Land of the Free: A Short History of the American People*. New York: Macmillan Company, 1947.

Moran, Charles. *The Sea of Memories: The Story of Mediterranean Strife, Past and Present*. New York: Scribner's Sons, 1942.

Mowat, Charles L. *East Florida as a British Province, 1763–1784*. Berkeley: University of California Press, 1943.

Reynolds, Charles B. *Old Saint Augustine; A Story of Three Centuries*. St. Augustine, 1885.

Romans, Bernard. *Natural History of East and West Florida*. New York, 1775.

Schopf, Johann David. *Travels in the Confederation, 1783– 1784*. Translated and edited by A.J. Morrison, Philadelphia, 1911.

Shortt, Adam, and Arthur G. Doughty. *Documents Relating to the Constitutional History of Canada, 1756–1783*. 2nd rev. ed., in two parts. Ottawa, 1918.

Siebert, Wilbur Henry. *Loyalists in East Florida, 1774–1785*. 2 Vols. Deland, Florida, 1929.

Van Doren, Mark, ed. *Travels of William Bartram*. New York: Dover Publications, 1959.

Articles

Mowat, Charles L. "That Odd Being De Brahm." *Florida Historical Quarterly*, XX (April, 1942), pp. 323–345.

Panagopoulos, E.P. "The Background of the Greek Settlers in the New Smyrna Colony." *Florida Historical Quarterly*, XXV, No. 2 (October, 1956) pp. 95–115.

Siebert, Wilbur H. "Slavery and White Servitude in East Florida, 1726–1776," *Florida Historical Quarterly*, X, No. 1 (July, 1931) p. 21.

Unpublished Material

Lawson, E. W. "Minorcans of St. Augustine." An unpublished paper read to Saint Augustine Historical Society. December 14, 1948.

About the Author

K enneth Henry Beeson Jr. was born in St. Augustine, Florida, in 1924. Educated by the Sisters of St. Joseph, he attended the University of Florida where he received a bachelor's degree in history and a master's degree in Latin American history.

He served in the United States Army during World War II and the Korean War and continued his military service with the Florida Army National Guard, retiring as a lieutenant colonel in 1976.

Beeson was a master tailor and owned a popular men's shop in St. Augustine for many years. He served as a commissioner for the city of St. Augustine and as the city's first elected mayor for two terms. He also taught courses in history at St. Johns River Community College from 1961 through 1991. Beeson was also a founder of The Sister Cities Association and The Menorcan Cultural Society.

In 2001 he was awarded St. Augustine's highest honor, the prestigious Order of La Florida for his many services to the community. Along with his wife, D. Louise (Lou), he raised four daughters: Karen Bromirski, the late Cheryl Beeson, Bonita Layfield and Alexis Beeson.

Kenny Beeson passed away in January of 2003, but he left behind a historical legacy for generations to come.

Alexis Beeson
St. Augustine, Florida
November 2005

www.ingramcontent.com/pod-product-compliance
Lightning Source LLC
Chambersburg PA
CBHW060815100426
42813CB00004B/1090